LIFTING UP OUR HEARTS
Praying with the Third Edition of the Roman Missal

Sign of Peace

Celebrant: The peace of the Lord be with you always.

All: And with your spirit.

Invitation to Communion

Celebrant: Behold the Lamb of God, behold him who takes away the sins of the world. Blessed are those called to the supper of the Lamb.

All: Lord, I am not worthy that you should enter under my roof, but only say the word and my soul shall be healed.

Concluding Rite

Celebrant: The Lord be with you.

All: And with your spirit.

Celebrant: May almighty God bless you, the Father, and the Son, ✠ and the Holy Spirit.

All: Amen.

Concluding Rite for a Pontifical Mass

Celebrant: The Lord be with you.

All: And with your spirit.

Celebrant: Blessed be the name of the Lord.

All: Now and for ever.

Celebrant: Our help is in the name of the Lord.

All: Who made heaven and earth.

Celebrant: May almighty God bless you, the Father, ✠ and the Son, ✠ and the Holy ✠ Spirit.

All: Amen.

D1450461

RENEW International
1232 George Street
Plainfield, NJ 07062-1717
www.renewintl.org

LUOH-PC

RENEW International fosters spiritual renewal in the Catholic tradition by empowering individuals and communities to encounter God in everyday life, deepen and share faith, and connect faith with action.

He will come again in glory
to judge the living and the dead
and his kingdom will have no end.

I believe in the Holy Spirit, the Lord,
the giver of life,
who proceeds from the Father and
the Son,
who with the Father and the Son
is adored and glorified,
who has spoken through the prophets.

I believe in one, holy, catholic and
apostolic Church.
I confess one Baptism for the
forgiveness of sins
and I look forward to the resurrection
of the dead
and the life of the world to come.
Amen.

Invitation to Pray

Celebrant: Pray my sisters and brothers.

All: May the Lord accept the
sacrifice at your hands
for the praise and glory of his
name,
for our good and the good of
all his holy Church.

Preface Dialogue

Celebrant: The Lord be with you.

All: And with your spirit.

Celebrant: Lift up your hearts.

All: We lift them up to the Lord.

Celebrant: Let us give thanks
to the Lord our God.

All: It is right and just.

Preface Acclamation (Holy, Holy, Holy)

All: Holy, Holy, Holy
Lord God of hosts.
Heaven and earth are
full of your glory.
Hosanna in the highest.
Blessed is he who comes
in the name of the Lord.
Hosanna in the highest.

Mystery of Faith (Memorial Acclamations)

Celebrant: The mystery of faith.

All: We proclaim your Death,
O Lord,
and profess your
Resurrection
until you come again.

Or:

All: When we eat this Bread and
drink this Cup,
we proclaim your Death,
O Lord,
until you come again.

Or:

All: Save us, Savior of the world,
for by your Cross and
Resurrection
you have set us free.

LIFTING UP OUR HEARTS
Praying with the Third Edition of the Roman Missal

Gloria

Glory to God in the highest,
and on earth peace to people
of good will.

We praise you,
we bless you,
we adore you,
we glorify you,
we give you thanks for your
great glory,
Lord God, heavenly King,
O God, almighty Father.

Lord Jesus Christ, Only Begotten Son,
Lord God, Lamb of God, Son of
the Father,
you take away the sins of the world,
have mercy on us;
you take away the sins of the world,
receive our prayer;
you are seated at the right hand of
the Father,
have mercy on us.

For you alone are the Holy One,
you alone are the Lord,
you alone are the Most High,
Jesus Christ,
with the Holy Spirit,
in the glory of God the Father.
Amen.

The Creed

I believe in one God,
the Father almighty,
maker of heaven and earth,
of all things visible and invisible.

I believe in one Lord Jesus Christ,
the Only Begotten Son of God,
born of the Father before all ages.
God from God, Light from Light,
true God from true God,
begotten, not made, consubstantial
with the Father;
through him all things were made.
For us men and for our salvation
he came down from heaven,

*At the words that follow, up to and
including* and became man, *all bow.*

and by the Holy Spirit was incarnate
of the Virgin Mary,
and became man.

For our sake he was crucified under
Pontius Pilate,
he suffered death and was buried,
and rose again on the third day
in accordance with the Scriptures.
He ascended into heaven
and is seated at the right hand of
the Father.

LIFTING UP OUR HEARTS
Praying with the Third Edition of the Roman Missal

The Greeting

Celebrant: The Lord be with you.

All: And with your spirit.

Penitential Act: Form A

**I confess to almighty God
and to you, my brothers and sisters,
that I have greatly sinned
in my thoughts and in my words,
in what I have done and in what I have
    failed to do,**

And, striking the breast, they say:

**through my fault, through my fault,
through my most grievous fault;**

Then they continue:

**therefore I ask blessed Mary
    ever-Virgin,
all the Angels and Saints,
and you, my brothers and sisters,
to pray for me to the Lord our God.**

Penitential Act: Form B

Celebrant: Have mercy on us, O Lord.

**All: For we have sinned
    against you.**

Celebrant: Show us, O Lord,
    your mercy.

**All: And grant us your
    salvation.**

Penitential Act: Form C

Celebrant: You were sent to heal
    the contrite of heart:
    Lord, have mercy.
    Or: *Kyrie, eleison.*

All: Lord, have mercy.
    Or: ***Kyrie, eleison.***

Celebrant: You came to call sinners:
    Christ, have mercy.
    Or: *Christe, eleison.*

All: Christ, have mercy.
    Or: ***Christe, eleison.***

Celebrant: You are seated at the
    right hand of the Father
    to intercede for us:
    Lord, have mercy.
    Or: *Kyrie, eleison.*

All: Lord, have mercy.
    Or: ***Kyrie, eleison.***

LIFTING UP OUR HEARTS

Praying with the
Third Edition of the Roman Missal

Peter J. Zografos

RENEW
INTERNATIONAL

RENEW International
1232 George Street
Plainfield, NJ 07062-1717
Phone: 908-769-5400
Fax: 908-769-5660
www.renewintl.org
www.renewintl.org/missal

✠ **NIHIL OBSTAT**
Monsignor James M. Cafone, S.T.D.
Censor Librorum

✠ **IMPRIMATUR**
Most Reverend John J. Myers, J.C.D., D.D.
Archbishop of Newark

Published with the approval of the Committee on Divine Worship, United States Conference of Catholic Bishops.

Cover and book design by Ruth Markworth

ISBN: 978-1-935532-52-1

Printed and bound in the United States of America

Contents

Appendix

Acknowledgments

The publisher gratefully acknowledges use of the following:

Excerpts from the English translation of *The Roman Missal* © 2010, International Commission on English in the Liturgy Corporation (ICEL); the English translation of the Psalm Responses from *Lectionary for Mass* © 1969, 1981, 1997, ICEL; the English translation the Prayer for Meetings from *A Book of Prayers* © 1982, ICEL; excerpt from the English translation of *Sacrosanctum Concilium* from *Documents on the Liturgy, 1963-1979: Conciliar, Papal, and Curial Texts* © 1982, ICEL. All rights reserved.

Scripture quotations from the *New Revised Standard Version Bible* (containing the Old and New Testaments with the Apocrophyal/Deuterocanonical Books) © 1989 by the Division of Christian Education of the National Council of the Churches of Christ in the U.S.A. and are used by permission. All rights reserved.

All papal and conciliar documents quoted in this book are from the English translations as presented by the Vatican website.

English translation of the *Catechism of the Catholic Church for the United States of America* © 1994, United States Conference of Catholic Bishops-Libreria Editrice Vaticana. English translation of the *Catechism of the Catholic Church: Modifications from the Editio Typica* © 1997, United States Conference of Catholic Bishops-Libreria Editrice Vaticana. Used with permission.

The United States Catholic Catechism for Adults © 2006 United States Conference of Catholic Bishops. Used with permission.

Foreword

At the time of the Second Vatican Council, the ongoing renewal of the liturgy introduced the use of the vernacular, new prayers and even some structural changes in the way that we celebrate the Eucharist. In the enthusiasm of those first days of renewal, there was a hastened introduction of the new Mass. Sometimes the changes were not always supported nor accompanied by appropriate formation. In some places there was little or no catechesis. It took time before many of the faithful finally received an explanation of any given particular change. We should not put blame anywhere. At the time, the resources for the average parish were quite limited. If someone did not have access to a theological library, the information was simply not accessible.

With the introduction of the *Third Edition of the Roman Missal*, promulgated by Pope John Paul II in the Jubilee Year 2000, and now officially translated into English, our situation is very different. There is a wealth of information on the Internet, and there are no significant ritual changes in the liturgy. The present moment is better, but the challenge remains. If today's catechesis to prepare for the praying of the new texts is to be as fruitful as possible, it should not simply be a "how-to" on the use of the texts. It should be more than just explaining certain word changes, such as the use of "consubstantial" in the Creed, or style changes, such as the structure of the Gloria.

> **❝ If today's catechesis to prepare for the praying of the new texts is to be as fruitful as possible, it should not simply be a "how-to" on the use of the texts ❞**

We are now given a special opportunity to deepen our appreciation of the gift of the liturgy itself. This is what *Lifting Up Our Hearts: Praying with the Third Edition of the Roman Missal* does. There are many resources available to help parishes implement the new Missal. What sets *Lifting Up Our Hearts* apart is that it is designed for parishioners' use in small faith-sharing groups, or what RENEW International calls "small Christian communities." Here we will gather for prayerful reflection on the new responses, their foundation in Sacred Scripture, and how participation in liturgy impacts our daily lives.

Through prayerful reflection and faith sharing, *Lifting Up Our Hearts* will help the faithful internalize the new liturgical responses thereby encouraging active, full, and conscious participation of the laity in the liturgy. It is not a well-known fact, but the words "the active participation of the laity" originated not with Vatican II, but with Pope Pius X. With his emphasis on music in the liturgy, he renewed the appreciation of the role of the laity in worship.

Pope Pius X urged the active participation of the faithful in the liturgy as the foremost and indispensable font of the true Christian spirit. He saw it as the place where the interior renewal of the Church begins.

With *Mediator Dei* in 1947, Pope Pius XII gave a new impetus to liturgical renewal, laying a path that moved toward Vatican II. He moved from a juridical notion of the Church as an institution to a more biblical and dynamic understanding of the Church as the Body of Christ. He reminded us that the Eucharist is at the heart of the Mystical Body, and he placed a renewed emphasis on the intelligible participation of the laity. It is precisely this idea of more active participation of the laity that has prompted the Church to publish a new Missal and its vernacular translations.

Since the first introduction of the vernacular, we have learned a few things. We have learned more about the scriptural and patristic sources of our liturgical texts, more about the vocabulary and its catechetical importance, and even more about the very art of translating. Based on this new understanding, *Liturgiam Authenticam* was promulgated in March 2001. It has been a helpful guide in the work on the new translations. The principles are clear and carefully thought out. However, in all fairness, it should be said that, as the principles were being applied, both the translators and the Holy See learned what worked and what did not work.

So, the new texts do follow *Liturgiam Authenticam* faithfully, but not rigidly. Translation is an art. And there must be respect for the receptor language. The new texts are good. They represent a development. They capture the wealth of the Church's theological vocabulary used in worship and, therefore, help us enter more fully into the riches of the liturgy itself.

> ❝ *Liturgy is the place where the Church herself is uniquely evangelized and becomes the community of believers whose faith is strong, whose hope is lively and whose charity is ardent* ❞

Our present moment of liturgical renewal is a graced moment for the very mission of the Church. The Church's mission is to evangelize. As Paul VI stated in *Evangelii Nuntiandi*, "Evangelizing is in fact the grace and vocation proper to the Church, her deepest identity. She exists in order to evangelize" (no. 14). For the Church to accomplish this mission that stems from the very activity of Jesus and the gift of the Holy Spirit, she herself begins by being evangelized. And how is the Church evangelized? She hears the Word, repents, and takes her nourishment from the Bread of Life. In a word, she enters into the liturgy.

Liturgy is the place where the Church herself is uniquely evangelized and becomes the community of believers whose faith is strong, whose hope is lively and whose charity is ardent. Liturgy is the place where the Church is called together again, like the Church in the Cenacle, and empowered by the Holy Spirit.

The new texts will have their place within this deepening of liturgical spirituality. And it is this wider context of liturgical catechesis and evangelization that we should keep always before us. The texts are a most privileged means for the Church to express the faith, to embrace the faith, and to pass on the faith. The texts, the liturgical rites, the liturgical year, the Scriptural readings, the preaching: the entire liturgy should stimulate our own continued conversion and growth in faith. There will be some challenge in adapting to the new texts. Translation is always an art, not a perfect science. The very fact that English is a living language means that this art evolves from one generation to the next.

We have come to an historic moment. After much collaboration on the international, national, and diocesan level, with clergy and laity, with experts and the faithful, after hours of discussion and debate, the new texts have been prepared. As the discussions and debates recede into the background, we now are able to receive the new texts with enthusiasm. The new translation has the potential, when unlocked through dynamic catechesis, to enrich spiritual lives and lead us to more active participation in the liturgical celebration. And the greater and more effective our liturgical celebration becomes, the more the Church will be energized to her essential work of evangelization of bringing Christ to the world and the world to Christ.

Most Reverend Arthur J. Serratelli, S.T.D., S.S.L., D.D.
Chairman, USCCB Committee on Divine Worship

Presenting RENEW International

The RENEW process, both parish-based and diocesan-wide, was first developed and implemented in the Archdiocese of Newark, New Jersey. Its success there led other dioceses, in the United States and in other countries, to bring RENEW to their people and parish communities. In the three decades since its vibrant beginnings, RENEW International has touched the lives of 25 million people in over 150 dioceses in the United States and 23 countries throughout the world.

RENEW International has grown organically from its original single RENEW process. Materials and training have been inculturated and made available in over 40 languages. We have added specific pastoral outreach to campuses and to young adults in their 20s and 30s. We have incorporated prison ministry and provided resources for the visually impaired.

The very core of all of these processes remains the same: to help people become better hearers and doers of the Word of God. We do this by encouraging and supporting the formation of small communities who gather prayerfully to reflect on and share the Word of God, to make better connections between faith and life, and to live their faith more concretely in family, work, and community life.

As a not-for-profit organization, our pastoral outreach is sustained in part from the sales of our publications and resources, and the stipends we receive for the services provided to parishes and dioceses. However, our priority is always to serve all parishes who desire to renew their faith and build the Church, regardless of their economic situation. We have been able to fulfill this mission not only in the inner city and rural areas in the United States but also in the developing world, especially Latin America and Africa, thanks to donations and charitable funding.

As you meet in your small group, we invite you to take a few moments to imagine the great invisible network of others, here in the United States and on the other continents. They gather, as you do, in small Christian communities, around the Word of God present in the Scripture, striving to hear and act upon that Word. Keep them in your prayer, a prayer of thanksgiving for the many graces we have experienced, a prayer that the Spirit will guide all of us as we lift up our hearts to the Lord and welcome the *Third Edition of the Roman Missal.*

Introduction

Our liturgical tradition has been preserved from the time of the Apostles through various written forms. The early Church fathers taught much about prayer. Presumably the oldest document of Church order, *The Didache* or *The Teaching of the Twelve Apostles* (c. 70-90), lays out detailed instructions as to how the Christian community is to form its prayer.

Our pattern of worship has evolved over the centuries. As Catholics we are very familiar with the format because our tradition uses a missal which contains the prayers and rubrics: how we do what we do. New editions of the Roman Missal, always written and published in Latin (as are all Church documents), were issued by eight popes between 1604 and 2002, and each maintained a consistent style of worship for prayer in the Roman Rite. Since the Second Vatican Council we have had two editions of the Roman Missal and now prepare to welcome the third edition. We will notice changes in language, but it will be the same Mass.

Over time there have been numerous liturgical changes. An era of liturgical reform often forgotten is the period from the Council of Trent (1563) to the advent of the Second Vatican Council (1963). The modern reform movement, beginning in the mid-nineteenth century and continuing for decades before Vatican II, is more than one hundred and fifty years old. While the early liturgical movement began as a romantic recovery of past traditions, this current renewal has become the impetus for the Church to engage the world in modern times as a sign of the reign of God. It has also led to a renewal of Christian faith and a renewed interest in unity among Christians.

Vatican II was the force for a renewed, intensive, and extensive study of the history of liturgy and prayer because the council asked the Church to recover its historical sources. *The Constitution on the Sacred Liturgy* states that history should serve as a guide for religious life and pastoral ministries and, therefore, liturgical reform (*Sacrosanctum Concilium*, 16, 23). Thus, the Second Vatican Council did more than call for the liturgical books to be translated into the vernacular; it restored the liturgy to the

"… the translation of the liturgical texts of the Roman Liturgy is not so much a work of creative innovation as it is of rendering the original texts faithfully and accurately into the vernacular language. While it is permissible to arrange the wording, the syntax and the style in such a way as to prepare a flowing vernacular text suitable to the rhythm of popular prayer, the original text, insofar as possible, must be translated integrally and in the most exact manner, without omissions or additions in terms of their content, and without paraphrases or glosses."

—ON THE USE OF VERNACULAR LANGUAGES IN THE PUBLICATION OF BOOKS OF THE ROMAN LITURGY (*LITURGIAM AUTHENTICAM*), 20

center of the life of the Church as the source and summit of the Christian life. In doing so, it continues to encourage the assembly to assume their proper liturgical role as ministers with full, active, and conscious participation in the Church and her liturgy.

Why a third edition?

The first edition of the Roman Missal was published April 1969 in Latin. By November, the U.S. bishops approved the English translation. The Vatican confirmed it for parish use the following January. Using the principle of "dynamic equivalence," Pope Paul VI's *Comme le Prévoit* (January 25, 1969) set the standard for all translation: to convey the essential meaning of the original text in the style and tone of the vernacular language. In 1971 the International Commission on English in the Liturgy (ICEL) began a consultation with the English-speaking bishops for a new translation of the missal. A survey of the bishops found overwhelming support for simple translations set in the style and tone of contemporary English. In November 1973 the U.S. bishops approved the newer ICEL translation, which was confirmed by the Holy See in February 1974. In 1975 the second edition of the Roman Missal was promulgated by Rome. It took ten years for this edition to be translated and approved so that in 1985 the second edition was published in English.

There were efforts to enhance and refine the earlier English translations by ICEL. In 1997 the U.S. bishops approved a new translation and submitted it to the Holy See in 1998. However, it was set aside because of Pope John Paul II's desire, as part of the Church's celebration of the Jubilee Year in 2000, to promulgate a third edition of the Roman Missal. The third edition would include the memorials of the new saints he canonized and would be published in Latin by 2002.

"That sound tradition may be retained, and yet the way remain open to legitimate progress careful investigation is always to be made into each part of the liturgy which is to be revised. This investigation should be theological, historical, and pastoral. Also the general laws governing the structure and meaning of the liturgy must be studied in conjunction with the experience derived from recent liturgical reforms and from the indults conceded to various places."

—CONSTITUTION ON THE SACRED LITURGY
(SACROSANCTUM CONCILIUM), 23

Why a new translation?

To prepare for the translations of the third edition, the Congregation for Divine Worship and the Discipline of the Sacraments (CDWDS) published *Liturgiam Authenticam* on the use of vernacular languages in the publication of the books of the Roman liturgy on March 28, 2001. It noted that translations of the liturgical texts in the various countries needed improvement through corrections or in many cases new translations.

There were some omissions or perhaps errors which affected the existing translations. Additionally, the Holy See created a new committee, *Vox Clara* (Latin for "clear voice"), to assist the CDWDS in facilitating the new norms for translation with ICEL and the English-speaking conferences of bishops.

Dynamic equivalence was set aside for a translation theory known as formal equivalence. New translations would follow the Latin syntax and vocabulary in order "to preserve the texts' dignity, beauty, and doctrinal precision." The new texts, which are in a higher linguistic register, require careful preparation for comprehensive proclamation. We will notice longer sentences that follow the Latin syntax along with a much broader and richer vocabulary. All of this will require us to listen attentively with new ears as the translation of the *Third Edition of the Roman Missal* adds variety to our expressions of liturgical prayer.

There has been considerable time for consultation and study of the new translation. The bishops of the English-speaking countries in consultation with ICEL and the CDWDS have been working on this for years. Now we have time to prepare to welcome the *Third Edition of the Roman Missal*. We have much to be thankful for while new insights into our sacred mysteries await us.

About the Author

Dr. Peter J. Zografos is a liturgical theologian, spiritual director, and community builder. He received a Doctor of Ministry Degree from Barry University, Miami; and a Master of Divinity Degree from the School of Theology and Ministry at Seattle University. He is an adjunct faculty member of the Graduate School of Theology and Ministry, Seattle University. Formerly director of Campus Ministry and an adjunct faculty member at Our Lady of the Lake University, San Antonio, Dr. Zografos also served as director of the Office of Evangelization and Worship for the Archdiocese of Anchorage. For the past year he has presented workshops on the *Third Edition of the Roman Missal* for the Federation of Diocesan Liturgical Commissions in partnership with the United States Conference of Catholic Bishops. He is a member of the Executive Committee of the FDLC and a member of the American Academy of Religion.

Faith Sharing in a Small Community

Welcome to *Lifting Up Our Hearts: Praying with the Third Edition of the Roman Missal.* Some of you have already experienced meeting and sharing in small communities. For others, this will be a new experience.

You are coming together as a group, but you are not just meeting as a discussion or study group where you talk about ideas. Rather, you gather in small Christian communities as a sharing group, open to the Spirit of God, seeking to grow in faith and in your relationship with God and one another.

For all of you engaging in this spiritual adventure together, here are some key ideas that help bring about good, healthy faith sharing.

Gathering

The first fundamental is that you have chosen to gather as a small community to share prayer, life, and faith in a way that will enrich your own lives, the life of your parish community, and the life of the diocese as a community. The members of the small group need to take the time to get to know one another. Always allow time for introductions at the first session. Then, at later sessions, take a moment or two to ask each other how you are and what has happened since you last met. If anyone new joins the group, again allow time for introductions. The goal is to form a community.

Hospitality and Environment

The right atmosphere is very important for faith sharing. The members of the group need to feel comfortable, physically and psychologically. Effective sharing needs a reflective atmosphere, with as few distractions as possible. It is good to establish a central focus, using a Bible, a candle, or similar visible sign that will help direct thoughts toward the theme of the session.

Timing

It is very important to get the timing of the session right. Under usual circumstances, a session should last 90 minutes. Most groups then extend their time together in a brief social. The time together in the session should have a balance of prayer, talking about your own experiences, exploring Scripture, reflection, faith sharing, and talking about ways of living out your faith. This balance is presented in more detail on pages xviii–xx.

Prayer

Prayer can and should take different forms. Invite different members of the group to lead the moments of prayer. Do not forget that silence is a very important part of any prayer, so build moments of quiet into the time of prayer with a gentle but explicit prompt from whoever is leading the prayer. For example: Let us spend a few moments in quiet, becoming more aware of God's presence, God's presence in each one of us, and especially in this community, gathered in Jesus' name.

Songs are suggested for the moments of prayer, and all of the songs listed in this book can be found on the *Lifting Up Our Hearts* CD. Lyrics to the songs are provided in the Appendix of this book.

However, these are only suggestions. If you can think of a more appropriate song, then you should substitute that for what we propose.

Scripture

Others before us read their experiences through the eyes of faith, and in those experiences saw the great story of God's loving relationship with his people. This is set out in what we call the Scriptures, the story God reveals to us, most of all through Christ his Son, the eternal Word. The faith-sharing session gives prominence to exploring Scripture, noticing what word, phrase, or image from it speaks to us. In a word, we share how Scripture has touched our hearts. We are offered input to help us understand what God is saying to us today. Then we reflect together on our experience, our story and God's story—and above all how the two link together. All are invited to reflect: each person who wishes to share his or her reflection aloud is given the opportunity to do so. No one dominates, and no one need talk unless he or she wants to.

Experience

Our spiritual lives do not exist without the events of our everyday lives! Our experience, then, is essential to our spiritual lives. We need to reflect on our story—what we have experienced in our families, in our other relationships—and explore how that relates to the theme of the session. You will notice that the reflections this book offers are sometimes expressed in the first person. This use of the first person is designed as a model for sharing, as an explicit encouragement to all of us to dare to say "I remember ..." and then to interpret that experience through the eyes of faith.

Challenge and Commitment

One of the key components of faith sharing is how we take what we hear and share and live it out in our lives. That is why a moment of challenge is built into every session. You are given the opportunity to respond, not just verbally, but by making a commitment to a clear and specific action that you see as a consequence of living out the faith expressed in the sharing. At the following meeting, you are invited to share how you did at living out that commitment.

We live in a hectic, busy world. Making time for outreach or action will not always be easy. The importance of this moment is the opportunity it gives you to reassess your priorities. The key question is not so much "Did I do what I said I would?" but rather "Through this activity, did I manage to live out my faith?" This should also make you look to the bigger question of living out your faith in the totality of your lives: in your family, in your other relationships, in your work environment. We may discover that rather than doing "more" it might be more important for you to do "less"! This is the time to look at how you are living the values of Jesus and the Gospel, and to identify what needs to change in your behaviors and attitudes.

Role of the Leader

Each small community will have its leader. In a faith-sharing context, the leader is not someone with all the answers who is there to preach or teach. The leader is a participant, with the particular responsibility of helping the group:

- by doing whatever is necessary to prepare for each session. It certainly involves reading over the session in advance so as to be totally at home with the reflection and questions. Preparing could also include delegating people to prepare the readings that will be used in the session; delegating the person who will lead the prayer; arranging and/or delegating others to plan and arrange the environment.

- by guiding the group through the faith-sharing process; by gently keeping the sharing focused on the theme of the session; and by moving the sharing from one moment to another, so that the balance and overall timing is respected.

- by listening, and by being prepared to ask questions that will keep the faith sharing moving yet focused.

- by ensuring that every participant who wants to speak has the opportunity to do so. More detailed suggestions for the leader are included in *Sowing Seeds: Essentials for Small Community Leaders*, which is available from RENEW International.

Faith-sharing Principles and Guidelines

The following guidelines will keep your faith-sharing community focused and help you to grow in faith, hope, and love.

Principles

- Faith is a gift from God. God leads each person on his or her spiritual journey. This happens in the context of the Christian community.

- Christ, the Word made flesh, is the root and foundation of Christian faith. It is because of Christ, and in and through him, that we come together to share our faith.

- "Faith sharing" refers to the shared reflections on the action of God in one's life experience as related to Scripture and the faith of the Church.

- Faith sharing is not discussion, problem solving, nor Scripture study. It is an opportunity for an encounter between a person in the concrete circumstances of his or her own life and a loving God, leading to a conversion of heart.

- The entire faith-sharing process is an expression of prayerful reflection.

Guidelines

- Constant attention to respect, honesty, and openness for each person will assist the community's growth.

- Each person shares on the level where he or she feels comfortable.

- Silence is a vital part of the total process. Participants are given time to reflect before any sharing begins, and a period of comfortable silence might occur between sharing by individual participants.

- Before sharing a second time, participants are encouraged to wait until all others who wish to do so have contributed.

- The entire community is responsible for participating and faith sharing.

- Confidentiality, which allows each person to share honestly, is essential.

- The natural culmination of the sharing should be the action commitment, the key to the spiritual growth of both individuals and community.

Suggestions for the Leader

You have the privilege of helping the small community to grow in a deeper awareness of God's dynamic presence in each member's life. Your own deep personal relationship with Jesus, through prayer and the sacraments and living your faith in your daily life, will help as you attempt to lead group members to richer prayer and transformative action. More detailed suggestions for the leader are included in *Sowing Seeds: Essentials for Small Community Leaders*. For more information, visit **www.renewintl.org/romanmissal**.

Preparation
Make a personal phone call to each member of the community in order to welcome him or her. Provide a way for each member to have a copy of this booklet at least a week before the first meeting. Invite the members to review the pew card and to read the Foreword, Introduction, designated Scripture reading, and reflections for the first session. At the end of each session, invite participants to prepare for the upcoming week by again reading the designated Scriptures and reflections.

Prior to the meeting time, prayerfully reflect upon the session. Preview the prayer suggestions. Prepare whatever is needed for prayer—music, words, equipment—or share this responsibility with another member of the group. On the day of the meeting, arrange the room for prayer and sharing.

It would be most helpful if some or all members of the group had Bibles at the meeting.

Time and Atmosphere
Each session should begin and end according to the schedule decided upon by the group. Create a relaxed atmosphere (suggestions for the environment are included). Be respectful and supportive of each member.

Loyalty to the Group
Remind the group of the obligation to keep all personal sharings confidential.

Refreshments
It is better to serve simple refreshments at the end of the session rather than at the beginning.

Sessions

Each session includes the following parts:

Introductions
If the group has not met before or if participants do not know each other, it is important to have time for introductions and an opportunity to get acquainted. People share most easily when they feel comfortable and accepted in a group.

Invitation to Pray

Each session begins with a time of prayer. Prayer must always be at the heart of gatherings of Christians. As leader, you need to decide how the opening prayer is conducted.

Living Our Faith

After the first week, the leader asks participants to share briefly how they did with their missioning response from the previous session. By reviewing these responses, participants encourage one another and hold one another accountable.

Reflection and Sharing

Each session contains two reflections on liturgy. The first reflection focuses on the new responses and the part of the Mass. The second reflection, which is about the connection between liturgy and Scripture and how liturgy impacts daily life, is followed by a series of faith-sharing questions. The reflections can be read aloud or silently. After reading the reflection, allow time for personal reflection before moving into the sharing questions. Allow sufficient time for all to share.

Praying the Roman Missal

Following the first reflection, participants will pray the new responses together.

Word of God

Following the first reflection and the praying of new liturgical responses, a key passage from Scripture is proclaimed. After a few minutes of silent reflection, the leader asks if anyone would like to share on the passage.

Missioning

Each session offers some ideas for an action; however, these are only suggestions. It is important that group members choose an action that is both measurable and realistic.

Sending Forth

The leader may use the suggested closing prayer or substitute another. When shared prayer is suggested, remember that praying spontaneously might be a new experience for some. Members should have the freedom to pray aloud or remain silent. Be comfortable with short periods of silence.

Structure and Flow of a Session

On pages xv–xvii, we presented some of the key elements that should be present for good, healthy faith sharing. We also talked about the importance of a balance. Here is another way of looking at a session, paying attention to the way it should be structured so that there is a natural flow, one part leading the participants to the next, deeper stage.

Having a structured routine frees the group from having to figure out "What do we do next?" It allows the members to concentrate on the what, rather than the how, to pay more attention to their inner selves and to the Word of God.

If you follow the suggested timings, a session will last approximately 90 minutes.

Gather [15 Minutes]

Elements

- Introductions [First time only or when a new person joins the group]
- Opening Prayer and Song Suggestion [5 minutes]
- Living Our Faith [10 minutes, sessions 2 through 6]

Purpose

- This is a sacred time. Enter it deliberately, as a community that has chosen to faith share together.
- Greet each other, consciously put yourselves in the presence of God, and pray for the grace to grow in faith.
- Share how the previous session has influenced your lives since you last met.
- The opening prayer and the song help to create a space for faith sharing.
- Focus on the theme of the session that is about to unfold.

Reflection 1 [5 Minutes]

Elements

- Short reflection on the new responses

Purpose

- This reflection provides catechesis on the new responses within the context of the Mass.

Praying the Roman Missal [5 minutes]

Elements

- Leader leads group in praying the new responses

Purpose

- This part gives participants the opportunity to pray the new responses aloud as part of a group.

Word of the Lord [20 minutes]

Elements

- Scripture reading [5 minutes]
- Moment of silent reflection and then invitation to brief sharing on the Scripture passage [5 minutes]
- A sharing question [10 minutes]

Purpose

- This part is about exploring "God's story" and in particular how it is speaking to us today.
- The question is designed to prompt sharing, which breaks open the Word of God in a way that helps participants connect Scripture to what happens in liturgy.

Reflection 2 [15 minutes]

Elements

- Reflection on the theme of the session connecting liturgy to daily life [5 minutes]
- Invitation to Share includes three or four questions on the theme of the session connecting liturgy to daily life [10 minutes]

Purpose

- This reflection is "our story" and helps participants come to a deeper understanding of the relationship between liturgy and life.
- Two or three questions to prompt sharing

Missioning [10 Minutes]

Elements

- Commitment to an action, and suggestions for actions

Purpose

- This part prompts the participants to understand that faith and faith sharing should impel you to commit to a specific and concrete act in the coming week, which flows from the sharing. This may be either a personal or a group action. Above all, it should be an action that, while challenging, is eminently doable.

- Suggestions, linked to the theme of the reflection, are offered by this book. These are secondary to actions that the group members discern as the fruit of your sharing.

Sending Forth [10 Minutes]

Elements

- Closing prayer consists of petitions, the Our Father, the Sign of Peace, and a closing song

Purpose

- The faith-sharing session concludes—as it began—in prayer.

Session One
THE LORD BE WITH YOU

Suggested Environment

A Bible, a candle, and other appropriate objects, such as a missalette or the pew card that accompanies Lifting Up Our Hearts, *may be arranged on a small table.*

Introductions

At this first session, if participants have not been together before, spend some time getting acquainted. A simple introduction of names and perhaps one thing they love about their faith could be shared.

Invitation to Pray

Leader: Let us put ourselves in the presence of God.

The group gives itself over to several moments of deepening silence as each member pays attention to her or his breathing, and slowly prays for stillness.

Leader: In the name of the Father, and of the Son, and of the Holy Spirit.

Pray together: **We stand before you, Holy Spirit,
conscious of our sinfulness,
but aware that we gather in your name.**

**Come to us, remain with us,
and enlighten our hearts.**

**Give us light and strength
to know your will,
to make it our own,
and to live it in our lives.**

**Guide us by your wisdom,
support us by your power,
for you are God,
sharing the glory of Father and Son.**

You desire justice for all:
enable us to uphold the rights of others;
do not allow us to be misled by ignorance
or corrupted by fear or favor.

Unite us to yourself in the bond of love
and keep us faithful to all that is true.

As we gather in your name
may we temper justice with love,
so that all our decisions
may be pleasing to you,
and earn the reward
promised to good and faithful servants.
Amen.

(This prayer was said before every session of Vatican II)

Song Suggestion

"Send Us Your Spirit," Dan Schutte (OCP)
See Appendix for lyrics.

"Mother Church earnestly desires that all the faithful should be led to that fully conscious, and active participation in liturgical celebrations which is demanded by the very nature of the liturgy. Such participation by the Christian people as 'a chosen race, a royal priesthood, a holy nation, a redeemed people' (1 Pt 2:9; see 2:4-5) is their right and duty by reason of their baptism."

—CONSTITUTION ON THE SACRED LITURGY (SACROSANCTUM CONCILIUM), 14

Reflection 1

We Gather in the Lord's Name

In the priest's greeting, "The Lord be with you," we are reminded that we gather in the name of Christ and that he is present in our gathering. When we respond, "And with your spirit," we acknowledge the mutual presence of the Holy Spirit in the assembly and the priest since we all received the Holy Spirit in the sacraments of initiation, which are baptism, confirmation, and Eucharist. St. John Chrysostom, in his Homily on the Holy Pentecost, teaches that our response, "And with your spirit," reminds all of us that the priest does nothing of his own power, but rather it is through the grace of the Holy Spirit that our sacraments are celebrated. It is Christ who always presides at our liturgy. Christ is present in the assembly, the person of ordained minister, in the Word proclaimed, and most especially in the body and precious blood of Christ. Christ's presence among us gives meaning and substance to our liturgies. We gather because we have been called by God to come together for the purpose of giving worship to God and creating communion with one another. We gather to be sent forth to work for the reign of God.

Most of us overlook the importance of the worshiping assembly to the liturgy. Often times as I visit various parishes I hear liturgical ministers greet each other by asking if they are "on" this Sunday or at this Mass. Of course we are always on! We all gather to perform the Ministry of the Assembly. Together with the priest, who is *in persona Christi in ecclesia* (in the person of Christ in the church), we fulfill Christ's command to gather and to do this in memory of him.

Praying the Greeting

> Leader:　Let us together pray the words of the Greeting.

> Leader:　The Lord be with you.
> **Response:　And with your spirit.**

"The Lord be with you"

"The Lord be with you" is a biblical greeting and can be found in:

- *Ruth 2:4* — "Just then Boaz came from Bethlehem. He said to the reapers, 'The Lord be with you.' They answered, 'The Lord bless you.'"

- *Judges 6:12* — "The angel of the Lord appeared to him and said to him, 'The Lord is with you, you mighty warrior.'"

- *2 Chronicles 15:2* — "He went out to meet Asa and said to him, 'Hear me, Asa, and all Judah and Benjamin: The Lord is with you, while you are with him. If you seek him, he will be found by you, but if you abandon him, he will abandon you."

- *Luke 1:28* — In the Gospels, the angel Gabriel says to Mary, "Greetings, favored one! The Lord is with you."

- *Matthew 28:20* — Jesus tells his disciples to remember that, "I am with you always, to the end of the age."

"And with your spirit"

The response, *"And with your spirit,"* is also biblical and may be found in letters written by or attributed to Paul:

- "The Lord be with your spirit," *2 Timothy 4:22*

- "May the grace of our Lord Jesus Christ be with your spirit, brothers and sisters. Amen," *Galatians 6:18*

- "The grace of the Lord Jesus Christ be with your spirit," *Philippians 4:23*

- "The grace of the Lord Jesus Christ be with your spirit," *Philemon 25*

The response *"And with your spirit"* is directed at individuals and also at entire church communities.

Word of the Lord

Leader selects one Scripture passage and asks a participant to proclaim it.
Ephesians 2:19-22 or **Colossians 3:11-17**

"To participate actively in the Mass, we need to resist a tendency to passivity when gathered in an audience-like setting. At Mass, we are an assembly of believers called to be a community joined in the praise and worship of God. We do this in the singing of hymns, psalms, recitation of prayers and responses, especially in our 'Yes' to God in the Great Amen. Active participation also requires an interior attention and a profound inner offering, as St. Paul urges in *Romans 12:1*: 'I urge you therefore, brothers, by the mercies of God to offer your bodies as a living sacrifice, holy and pleasing to God, your spiritual worship.'

When the assembly of the faithful, from the hands of the priest, offers the sacrifice of Christ to the Father, the members of the assembly are called to offer their bodies as a living sacrifice, holy and pleasing to God. In using the word *body*, St. Paul does not mean simply our flesh and bones, but rather our very selves. This, then, is a spiritual sacrifice."

—**UNITED STATES CATECHISM FOR ADULTS, PP. 225-226**

Silent Reflection

What word, phrase, or image from the Scripture reading touches my heart or speaks to my life? Reflect on this quietly or share it aloud.

Sharing Question

- How do you experience being a member of the body of Christ?

Reflection 2
The Work of the People of God

The council fathers recovered the ancient understanding that liturgy is our participation in the work of God. We can pray by ourselves but we cannot do liturgy by ourselves. For liturgy, our participation in an assembly of the faithful is optimal. Praying together is one of the ways we cooperate with God's plan for creation. The Catholic faith has always embraced creation—water, air, light, darkness, the beauty of the earth; work of human hands in the bread and wine; oil and incense and the light of candles—and used its elements in worship. We lift up our hands and heart to the One who has created the very things about which we speak words of thanks and praise. As a baptized people, we stand in awe as we pray, realizing, with St. Paul, that we have access to God through the gifts of creation declared by God to be "very good."

The Church over the centuries has used these gifts of creation to help us lift up our hearts together in prayer and has called it liturgy. The U.S. bishops have stated, "Liturgy is the source of the Church's prayer and action, and the summit by which our lives and all our ministries ascend to the Father" (*Sing to the Lord: Music in Divine Worship*, 2007, Foreword). Thus, we are called into full, conscious, and active participation at Mass. Our participation involves five fundamental actions: gathering, listening, giving thanks, praying and singing, and going forth. These are the gifts that we give to each other. What we do together expresses the reality that we are sisters and brothers in Christ.

We as Catholics do not invent our worship services; we don't improvise our liturgies. With the exception of the hymns, brief introductions, the homily, and the prayers of the faithful, most of the words sung or spoken during Mass are given to us in the liturgical books: the Roman Missal and the Lectionary. So we are called to prepare rather than plan. We prepare to use properly the appropriate texts that are given to us for the specific celebration. We prepare to have our prayers summed up in the words of the Collect (prayers that are given for a particular day that the priest celebrant offers in the name of the whole liturgical assembly). We prepare to hear the Word through the words of the Scripture readings given for the day in the Lectionary (the book of readings). And through all of this careful preparation of the liturgy which has been given to us, God can take us by surprise when we least expect it through our prayerful liturgical celebrations.

All ritual involves familiar words and actions, things everyone knows. Our liturgical prayer has fixed patterns. When we hear "through Christ, our Lord" we automatically reply "Amen." The familiar set of words or gestures evokes a familiar response. This expresses well the dialogue format, the "call and response" nature of the Mass. This dialogue between the liturgical assembly and its ministers reflects the dialogue between God and his people.

It is our responsibility to make these words, which we say by heart, become words that truly come from the heart. The Church believes as she prays. The ancient saying, *lex orandi, lex credendi*, means "we pray as we believe." The rule of prayer is the rule of faith: Liturgy is a constitutive element of the holy and living Tradition. With this new edition of the Roman Missal we have an opportunity to hear the words with a new heart and thus gain a deeper understanding of our faith so as to share what we have received.

> "As the work of Christ liturgy is also an action of his *Church*. It makes the Church present and manifests her as the visible sign of the communion in Christ between God and men. It engages the faithful in the new life of the community and involves the 'conscious, active, and fruitful participation' (*Sacrosanctum Concilium*, 11) of everyone."
>
> —**CATECHISM OF THE CATHOLIC CHURCH**, 1071

Invitation to Share

- In the liturgy, Christ is present in the person of the ordained minister, the assembly, the Word and the Eucharist. In which of these do I most easily experience Christ, and why?
- How do I sense or experience the work of the Holy Spirit in the liturgy?
- As a person in the pew, how do I participate fully, consciously and actively?
- Why is it important that I respond aloud in song and word?

Missioning

Determine a specific action (individual or group) that flows from your sharing. This should be your primary consideration for choosing an action. If choosing an individual action, determine what you will do and share it with the group. If choosing a group action, determine who will take responsibility for different aspects of the action.

The following are secondary suggestions:

- Prepare for next Sunday's liturgy by prayerfully reading and reflecting on the Scripture readings during the week. The readings can be found on the U.S. Conference of Catholic Bishops' website, www.usccb.org/nab/
- During the week, take note of how the signs and symbols of Sunday liturgy (bread, wine, water, light, etc.) are found and used in daily life.
- For more on the celebration of liturgy in the sacraments, see the *United States Catechism for Adults*, Chapter 14, "The Celebration of the Paschal Mystery," and Chapter 17, "The Eucharist: The Source and Summit of the Christian Life."

Sending Forth

The leader invites the people to think about all they have heard and experienced during the session.

> Leader: As we come to our closing prayer, for whom do we pray, and what do we pray for this night?

Participants offer individual petitions to which all respond "The Lord be with you."
Conclude with the Our Father, the Sign of Peace, and the closing song.

Sign of Peace

> Leader: The peace of the Lord be with you always.
> **Response: And with your spirit.**

Song Suggestion

"Send Out Your Spirit," Jesse Manibusan (OCP)
See Appendix for lyrics.

Next Steps

Prepare for your next session by prayerfully reading and studying:

- Session 2: "Have Mercy on Us, O Lord"
- Nehemiah 1:5-9
- Visit the U.S. Conference of Catholic Bishops' website about the Roman Missal and review the Frequently Asked Questions and Answers, www.usccb.org/romanmissal/faqs2.shtml
- If you haven't done so already, read the Foreword and Introduction on pages v–xi, which contain important background information about the *Third Edition of the Roman Missal*.

Session Two

HAVE MERCY ON US, O LORD

Suggested Environment

A Bible, a candle, and other appropriate objects, such as a missalette or the pew card that accompanies Lifting Up Our Hearts, *may be arranged on a small table.*

Invitation to Pray

Leader: Let us put ourselves in the presence of the Lord.

The group gives itself over to several moments of deepening silence as each member pays attention to her or his breathing, and slowly prays for stillness.

Leader: In the name of the Father, the Son and the Holy Spirit.

Pray together: **We stand before you, Holy Spirit,
conscious of our sinfulness,
but aware that we gather in your name.**

**Come to us, remain with us,
and enlighten our hearts.**

**Give us light and strength
to know your will,
to make it our own,
and to live it in our lives.**

**Guide us by your wisdom,
support us by your power,
for you are God,
sharing the glory of Father and Son.**

**You desire justice for all:
enable us to uphold the rights of others;
do not allow us to be misled by ignorance
or corrupted by fear or favor.**

**Unite us to yourself in the bond of love
and keep us faithful to all that is true.**

> **As we gather in your name**
> **may we temper justice with love,**
> **so that all our decisions**
> **may be pleasing to you,**
> **and earn the reward**
> **promised to good and faithful servants.**
> **Amen.**

(This prayer was said before every session of Vatican II)

Song Suggestion

 "Be Merciful, O Lord – Misericordia, Señor (Ps 51/50)," World Library Publications/J.S.Paluch Company. *See Appendix for lyrics.*

Living Our Faith

Share briefly your experience of putting into effect the action you chose after the last session.

"Certain words that may appear to have been introduced into the Latin liturgical text for reasons of meter or other technical or literary reasons convey, in reality, a properly theological content, so that they are to be preserved, insofar as possible, in the translation. It is necessary to translate with the utmost precision those words that express aspects of the mysteries of faith and the proper disposition of the Christian soul. Certain expressions that belong to the heritage of the whole or of a great part of the ancient Church, as well as others that have become part of the general human patrimony, are to be respected by a translation that is as literal as possible, as for example the words of the people's response *Et cum spiritu tuo*, or the expression *mea culpa, mea culpa, mea maxima culpa* in the Act of Penance of the Order of the Mass."

—*Liturgiam Authenticam*, 55-56

Reflection 1

God Is Good

There is a call often heard within the African-American church: "God is good!" To which the assembly responds: "All the time!" The leader then responds: "All the time." And the assembly concludes: "God is good." Thus both proclaim the whole truth but need each other for the sum, so that the sum is greater than the parts.

As members of the body of Christ we experience the outpouring of the gratuitous gift of God's love. In the light of this love we become aware of our faults and failings and how our sinfulness weakens the community. Aware that we are unworthy to celebrate the Eucharist, we ask for God's forgiveness as a community. The Penitential Rite is more than individuals coming together to acknowledge individual sin; it is a public communal acknowledgment of sin. Individual confession is between the individual and God; the Penitential Rite is about us and God. The relationship between liturgy and the life all around us is the profound and incarnate expression of our faith. Liturgy is not where we go to avoid the world, retreat from the mundane, or recoil from life. Liturgy is where we bring our shattered dreams of crushed lives, our lamentations of loss, our sorrows, and the pain of a broken world. We also bring our joys and hopes knowing that through the celebration of the Paschal Mystery all is transformed.

The Gospel stories we hear proclaimed at Mass contain a very compelling bias: the warp of the tapestry of Christ's life and mission woven together with God's love. The Gospel call is a radical option for the poor, the disenfranchised, the abused, the oppressed, the powerless, the unheard voice, those who have no voice, and those who do not receive a share of God's creation: the resources of the world. To deny or to ignore this bias is not an option for the Christian. This bias must be the community's starting point in preparing and celebrating the liturgy, especially in hearing the Word of God and offering its prayers to God.

> ❝ *Liturgy is about getting life right rather than getting the rite right* ❞

Jesus said: "I give you a new commandment, that you love one another. Just as I have loved you, you also should love one another. By this everyone will know that you are my disciples, if you have love for one another" (John 13:34-35). Christ's command to love God and love each other makes a claim on the individual and more importantly on the community assembled. It makes us responsible for all of creation and, therefore, all members of the human family. A commitment to the disenfranchised is also a commitment to systemic change, so that they too can gain access to the unlimited possibilities of the world and thus live as the heirs to God's abundant creation.

There is a danger that we do the right thing for the wrong reason. Liturgy forbids us to become trapped in doing actions as religious behavior to feel good while overlooking the mystery to which liturgy points. Liturgy is inauthentic when it becomes disconnected from the world and does not impel us to action. We must never be satisfied with externals, but rather allow them to lead us in our search for God found always and everywhere, who is the source of all our prayer and our longing. Liturgy is about getting life right rather than getting the rite right.

Praying the Penitential Rite

Leader: Brothers and sisters, let us acknowledge our sins, and so prepare ourselves to celebrate the sacred mysteries.

Penitential Act: Form A

I confess to almighty God
and to you, my brothers and sisters,
that I have greatly sinned
in my thoughts and in my words,
in what I have done and in what I have failed to do,

And, striking the breast, they say:
through my fault, through my fault,
through my most grievous fault;

Then they continue:
therefore I ask blessed Mary ever-Virgin,
all the Angels and Saints,
and you, my brothers and sisters,
to pray for me to the Lord our God.

Penitential Act: Form B

Leader: Have mercy on us, O Lord.
Response: For we have sinned against you.
Leader: Show us, O Lord, your mercy.
Response: And grant us your salvation.

Word of the Lord

Leader asks a participant to proclaim the Scripture passage.
Nehemiah 1:5-9

Silent Reflection

What word, phrase, or image from the Scripture reading touches my heart or speaks to my life? Reflect on this quietly or share it aloud.

Sharing Question

• Nehemiah speaks of the sinfulness of his community, Israel. In what ways is our Penitential Rite at Mass similar to Nehemiah's prayer?

Reflection 2

God Is Love

There is an ancient African saying: "A person is a person because of other persons." This wisdom is evident every time we gather with our sisters and brothers at Mass. Consider the ways that our liturgical prayer reconnects us to spiritual companionship; after all, we are Christians together, not apart. Our communal prayers—the Penitential Rite, the intercessory prayers, the Mystery of Faith (Memorial Acclamations)—have the potential to make us a holy, welcoming, and inclusive people. Prayer as hospitality and mercy calls us to heal the wounded and alienated in our communities. The Gospel impels faith communities to look inward and outward and to reach beyond limited perceptions of who merits the good news and who is welcome. We must reach out to all those who are marginalized: divorced and separated persons, persons with disabilities, the stranger among us, the abandoned, and the homeless.

The good news of the Gospel is that God is love. Given that kind of abundant love, which enfolds, supports, and sustains us, can anything such as sickness or sorrow, an opponent or obstacle, even death or despair separate us as members of God's family? God's call is for our cooperation and participation in love as a family. If God gave the ultimate gift of his self in Jesus for the sake of all, then is there anything that God would deny us? It is overwhelming to realize that there is one thing that you and I have in common with Christ: we are all God's family!

Becoming, welcoming, and including all are the hallmarks of the Christian community's home between the present and the promised future. Becoming, welcoming, and including all are the characteristics of the "now and not yet" of the kingdom. Becoming, welcoming, and including all are rooted in and spring from hospitality. Jesus' ministry was first about a hospitality that honored the dignity of all. Can Christian communities become anything less than hospitable, welcoming, and inclusive? It is only from this place of welcoming that our faith can do justice. An inclusive community more clearly points to the obligations of a priestly people to work for social justice and recaptures the practice of journeying in faith with others.

> "But in order that the liturgy may be able to produce its full effects, it is necessary that the faithful come to it with proper dispositions, that their minds should be attuned to their voices, and that they should cooperate with divine grace lest they receive it in vain. Pastors of souls must therefore realize that, when the liturgy is celebrated, something more is required than the mere observation of the laws governing valid and licit celebration; it is their duty also to ensure that the faithful take part fully aware of what they are doing, actively engaged in the rite, and enriched by its effects"
>
> —CONSTITUTION ON THE SACRED LITURGY (SACROSANCTUM CONCILIUM), 11

As a "feel good" society we seem to avoid the other side of the "good life," that is, the painful things: our sins of commission and our sins of omission both individually and as a society. This is often mirrored in our liturgical life. However, the individual members of the body of Christ must ask tough questions of our culture and our religious families of faith. How do I contribute to injustice in the world by my decisions? How is sin active in my own life? Am I aware that every personal decision I make is a moral decision? How have my preconceived ideas about others prevented me from seeing, knowing, and loving them? Who is missing from our assembly? Whom have we excluded from the table? These questions have the power to reveal the meaning of sin in our lives. Only when that has been revealed can the community begin to think about sin differently. Only then can the community begin to form its prayers differently. Faith that does justice requires a direct correspondence between the public worship of the church and the prayerful consciousness of the local church community. With consciousness raised we become more attentive and intentionally welcoming and inclusive.

> ❝ *When our daily struggles and trials cause us to lose focus, Christ's words of love and mercy can help us regain our perspective* ❞

God so loves each of us and gathers us again and again to share love and family. When our daily struggles and trials cause us to lose focus, Christ's words of love and mercy can help us regain our perspective. God is always calling us back home to the family. We experience families in different sizes, shapes, and types during our lifetimes. We have family through blood lines, families that are blended because of marriage, families that are adopted, intentional families, the human family. And most of us also seek one family: God's family. God's love bonds us into one community as an extended loving family. Through this infusion of divine love, God gives each of us the power of all of us, united in love.

As we will prepare to welcome the *Third Edition of the Roman Missal*, study of liturgical prayer in the coming weeks will help parish communities to restore the hopeful and prayerful anticipation that was present at that first gathering in the Upper Room at Pentecost, where everyone was welcomed. Together we are challenged to go beyond our own limits of inclusion and justice-making.

Invitation to Share

- What are the messages from society that are contrary to the Gospel message?
- As a church community, for what do we need to ask and accept forgiveness?
- How have I experienced God's mercy?
- How does our current celebration of liturgy help build the reign of God?

Missioning

Determine a specific action (individual or group) that flows from your sharing. This should be your primary consideration for choosing an action. If choosing an individual action, determine what you will do and share it with the group. If choosing a group action, determine who will take responsibility for different aspects of the action

The following are secondary suggestions:

- Prepare for next Sunday's liturgy by prayerfully reading and reflecting on the Scripture readings during the week. The readings can be found on the U.S. Conference of Catholic Bishops' website, www.usccb.org/nab/

- The next time you attend Mass, look around to see who is alone or new to the parish. Make a point of introducing yourself and welcoming them to the parish.

- Does your parish have a hospitality committee? If so, consider joining. If not, ask your pastor if you can start one.

Sending Forth

The leader invites the people to think about all they have heard and experienced during the session.

> Leader: As we come to our closing prayer, for whom do we pray, and what do we pray for this night?

Participants offer individual petitions to which all respond, "Have mercy on us, O Lord."

Conclude with the Our Father, the Sign of Peace, and the closing song.

Sign of Peace

> Leader: The peace of the Lord be with you always.
> **Response: And with your spirit.**

Song Suggestion

"Lord, Show Us Your Mercy and Love," Janet Sullivan Whitaker (OCP)
See Appendix for lyrics.

Next Steps

Prepare for your next session by prayerfully reading and studying:

- Session 3: "You Alone Are the Lord"
- Luke 2:13-14; and Romans 8
- Additional scriptural references: Revelation 4:11, 5:11-14

Session Three

YOU ALONE ARE THE LORD

Suggested Environment

A Bible, a candle, and other appropriate objects, such as a missalette or the pew card that accompanies Lifting Up Our Hearts, *may be arranged on a small table.*

Invitation to Pray

Leader: Let us put ourselves in the presence of the Lord.

The group gives itself over to several moments of deepening silence as each member pays attention to her or his breathing, and slowly prays for stillness.

Leader: In the name of the Father, the Son and the Holy Spirit.

Pray together: **We stand before you, Holy Spirit,
conscious of our sinfulness,
but aware that we gather in your name.**

**Come to us, remain with us,
and enlighten our hearts.**

**Give us light and strength
to know your will,
to make it our own,
and to live it in our lives.**

**Guide us by your wisdom,
support us by your power,
for you are God,
sharing the glory of Father and Son.**

**You desire justice for all:
enable us to uphold the rights of others;
do not allow us to be misled by ignorance
or corrupted by fear or favor.**

**Unite us to yourself in the bond of love
and keep us faithful to all that is true.**

As we gather in your name
may we temper justice with love,
so that all our decisions
may be pleasing to you,
and earn the reward
promised to good and faithful servants.
Amen.

(This prayer was said before every session of Vatican II)

Song Suggestion

"You Alone" Sarah Hart, Dwight Liles (OCP)
See Appendix for lyrics.

"Nevertheless the liturgy is the summit toward which the activity of the Church is directed; at the same time it is the font from which all her power flows. For the aim and object of apostolic works is that all who are made sons of God by faith and baptism should come together to praise God in the midst of His Church, to take part in the sacrifice, and to eat the Lord's supper. The liturgy in its turn moves the faithful, filled with 'the paschal sacraments,' to be 'one in holiness'; it prays that 'they may hold fast in their lives to what they have grasped by their faith'; the renewal in the Eucharist of the covenant between the Lord and man draws the faithful into the compelling love of Christ and sets them on fire. From the liturgy, therefore, and especially from the Eucharist, as from a font, grace is poured forth upon us; and the sanctification of men in Christ and the glorification of God, to which all other activities of the Church are directed as toward their end, is achieved in the most efficacious possible way."

—**Constitution on the Sacred Liturgy**
(**Sacrosanctum Concilium**), 10

Living Our Faith

Share briefly your experience of putting into effect the action you chose after the last session.

Reflection 1

God Is for Us

One of my favorite practical theologians was quoted as once saying, "Too much of a good thing is wonderful!" I am sure that she was speaking of God's love and grace as expressed in this wonderful angelic hymn that we sing on Sundays and major solemnities. The *Gloria* has been part of our Mass since the ninth century and has been in the morning prayer of the Eastern Church since about the third century. The *Gloria* is also known as the Great Doxology because of its Trinitarian formula.

"Glory to God" expresses the biblical notion that all creation comes to its fullness in God through Christ. Thus it is really a hymn about the abundance of God. This notion can also be found in the Hebrew Scriptures (Exodus 3:5) and in the Christian Scriptures (Romans 8). Paul's words, "If God is for us, who can be against us?" point to the sure hope of our destiny in the fullness in the life of the glory of God. He assures us that God is God-with-us (*Emmanuel*) and also God is for us! Given that kind of loving grace—which enfolds, supports, and sustains—can anything, any challenge, any opponent or obstacle deter us as God's people? Paul also gives us an impassioned testimony to Christ's unconditional love and acceptance, which is without parallel. If God gave the ultimate gift of his self in Jesus for the sake of all, then is there anything that God would deny to humankind? God actually proved and continues to prove his abundant, inexhaustible love for us, through Jesus Christ and the grace and peace of the Holy Spirit.

St. Paul plays the devil's advocate cross-examining the Church of Rome with a series of questions: "Who will bring any charge against God's elect?" (Romans 8:33); "Who is to condemn? (Romans 8:34); "Who will separate us from the love of God? Will hardship, or distress, or persecution, or famine, or nakedness, or peril, or sword?" (8:35). The answers to these questions are found in the *Gloria*, the history of salvation. God has already acquitted us of all sin and continues to love us. Our contemporary culture might say, "Awesome!" but we can say, "God is good!"

The Holy Spirit, the Paraclete, is our advocate helping us, guiding us, teaching us, counseling us, and empowering us. The English poet William Blake wrote, "We are put on earth for a little space, that we may learn to bear the beams of love." When our daily struggles and trials cause us to lose focus, Paul's hymn and the *Gloria* will help us regain our perspective. God is for us! Who can be against us? So let's not muddy the experience. It is as simple as "Too much of a good thing is wonderful!"

Praying the Gloria

Leader: Let us together pray the *Gloria*.

Glory to God in the highest,
and on earth peace to people of good will.

We praise you,
we bless you,
we adore you,
we glorify you,
we give you thanks for your great glory,
Lord God, heavenly King,
O God, almighty Father.

Lord Jesus Christ, Only Begotten Son,
Lord God, Lamb of God, Son of the Father,
you take away the sins of the world,
     have mercy on us;

> **you take away the sins of the world,**
>   **receive our prayer;**
> **you are seated at the right hand of the Father,**
>   **have mercy on us.**
>
> **For you alone are the Holy One,**
> **you alone are the Lord,**
> **you alone are the Most High,**
> **Jesus Christ,**
> **with the Holy Spirit,**
> **in the glory of God the Father.**
> **Amen.**

Word of the Lord

Leader asks a participant to proclaim the Scripture passage.
Luke 2:13-14

Silent Reflection

What word, phrase, or image from the Scripture reading touches my heart or speaks to my life? Reflect on this quietly or share it aloud.

Sharing Question

• How do I experience the glory of God?

Reflection 2

We Are for God

There is a second-century quotation from Irenaeus, one of the church's first theologians: "The Glory of God is the human person fully alive."

In my ministry to persons with AIDS I learned that to journey with another is to walk with God. I was on holy ground in those silent moments when I could only sit there helpless, having no answers, listening to the pain of Andrew, a young man dying. My life changed forever. I found that our lives gave glory to God in those intimate moments of silent witness. I entered the mystery of God's glory as companion to another's life and death.

"The Word of God was made human in order that we might be made divine."

—**Athanasius,**
4th century

My life has been a journey wherein I found my way through the questions I asked. How was I taught to seek the answers? The Jesuits formed me as a young man, and the *ratio studiorum* (Latin for "plan for studies") guided my teachers and, therefore, my education. My soul was formed in the same logical manner.

The Baltimore Catechism, a "rules of the road" book to heaven, formed my youthful spirituality. I was fed all the answers but never invited to ask the questions. I had to discover the questions to which the answers are attainable only through God's abundant gift of grace. It is the same God who showers us with unquestionable mercy. Grace is a gift of God's glory and presence. Every person and moment is graced, since God's grace is always freely offered.

The glory of God is more evident each time we step outside of ourselves. God often enters into our life and interferes with our expectations and it is there that we find God with us and in us. We are enriched when we take the time to look for and appreciate all those apparent interruptions as a part of the gift of life, wherein we find the mystery of the glory of God.

Truth in our modern world is hard to discern. It is more comforting to say, "Eureka, I have it!" When we think we have it, we cease the quest. Perhaps it is more important to form the questions rather than just look for the easy answers. Secure in the knowledge that God is for us, we are capable of asking questions. Perhaps that is part of being fully human and fully alive.

> ❝ *I pray not that God is in my life, but that my life is in God* ❞

Called into a relationship with God we are naturally open to God and become more fully human as our relationship deepens. Human relationships are important because of the presence of God within them. We seek relationships because we seek God.

When we are open to the seeming inconveniences and to the diversions along the way, we can find the glory of God. Ultimately, it is in those quiet and often mundane moments that we meet ourselves: fully alive. The ultimate stance before God is silence. It is there that I meet God. It is in that silence that we can hear the heavenly hymn: Glory to God. I pray not that God is in my life, but that my life is in God!

Invitation to Share

- We just reflected on the importance of questions in the faith journey. What are the questions that have brought me closer to God?

- Share an experience of entering into the mystery of God's glory.

- How does my life glorify God?

Missioning

Determine a specific action (individual or group) that flows from your sharing. This should be your primary consideration for choosing an action. If choosing an individual action, determine what you will do and share it with the group. If choosing a group action, determine who will take responsibility for different aspects of the action.

The following are secondary suggestions:

- Prepare for next Sunday's liturgy by prayerfully reading and reflecting on the Scripture readings during the week. The readings can be found on the U.S. Conference of Catholic Bishops' website, www.usccb.org/nab/

- Read and reflect on the *Gloria* while listening to the "Alleluia Chorus" in Handel's "Messiah." Go to www.youtube.com and search for "Alleluia Chorus" as recorded by the Opera Company of Philadelphia on Oct. 30, 2010.

Sending Forth

The leader invites the people to think about all they have heard and experienced during the session.

> Leader: As we come to our closing prayer, for whom do we pray,
> and what do we pray for this night?

Participants offer individual petitions and all respond, "You alone are the Lord."

Conclude with the Our Father, the Sign of Peace, and the closing song.

Sign of Peace

> Leader: The peace of the Lord be with you always.
> **Response: And with your spirit.**

Song Suggestion

 "Glory to God," from the revised *Mass of Glory*, Ken Canedo and Bob Hurd (OCP) *See Appendix for lyrics.*

Next Steps

Prepare for your next session by prayerfully reading and studying:

- Session 4: "I Believe"

- John 20:24-29; also Mark 9:24; John 11:27; and 1 John 5:10

- The Athanasian Creed, traditionally ascribed to St. Athanasius (296-373). Like other creeds, such as the Apostles' Creed, it is a profession of the Christian faith, but it is also a full-fledged theology lesson, making it the longest of the creeds. Athanasius spent his life combating the Arian heresy, which denied the divinity of Christ by denying that there are three Persons in one God. The Athanasian Creed may be found at: http://www.newadvent.org/cathen/02033b.htm

- Acts of the Apostles on the conflicts regarding faith that arose in the early church (e.g., Acts 15:1-35)

Session Four
I BELIEVE

Suggested Environment

A Bible, a candle, and other appropriate objects, such as a missalette or the pew card that accompanies Lifting Up Our Hearts, *may be arranged on a small table.*

Invitation to Pray

Leader: Let us put ourselves in the presence of the Lord.

The group gives itself over to several moments of deepening silence as each member pays attention to her or his breathing, and slowly prays for stillness.

Leader: In the name of the Father, the Son and the Holy Spirit.

Pray together: **We stand before you, Holy Spirit,**
conscious of our sinfulness,
but aware that we gather in your name.

Come to us, remain with us,
and enlighten our hearts.

Give us light and strength
to know your will,
to make it our own,
and to live it in our lives.

Guide us by your wisdom,
support us by your power,
for you are God,
sharing the glory of Father and Son.

You desire justice for all:
enable us to uphold the rights of others;
do not allow us to be misled by ignorance
or corrupted by fear or favor.

Unite us to yourself in the bond of love
and keep us faithful to all that is true.

> **As we gather in your name**
> **may we temper justice with love,**
> **so that all our decisions**
> **may be pleasing to you,**
> **and earn the reward**
> **promised to good and faithful servants.**
> **Amen.**
>
> *(This prayer was said before every session of Vatican II)*

Song Suggestion

"If You Believe and I Believe" (OCP)
See Appendix for lyrics.

Living Our Faith

Share briefly your experience of putting into effect the action you chose after the last session.

Reflection 1

Already and Not Yet

Liturgy is the place were we encounter both *kairos* and *chronos* time: the now and not yet of the kingdom. It is the meeting place for the assembly of the baptized and those seeking baptism. It is the welcoming place of inclusion where the afflicted can be comforted and the missioning place where the comfortable should be afflicted by the word proclaimed and prayed.

In the Creed, we stand together as one people as we proclaim one faith and one baptism. With the introduction of the *Third Edition of the Roman Missal*, we will each make that declaration of faith in the first person. I can only witness to what I believe, but together our witness is greater than the sum of the parts. Thus, in the liturgical act the "I" becomes "we" as we proclaim it together. The change is also an invitation for each of us to reflect upon what we each believe without the assumption of "we."

> **❝ ...to tell the story of the Son is to tell the story of God. We come to know God through the life of the Son, God in our midst ❞**

The Creed we recite is actually the Nicene-Constantinopolitan Creed. The bishops of the world assembled at Nicea in the year 325 to resolve their differences with Arius. Arius was a priest who, using reason to shape faith, claimed that Jesus could not be both human and divine. The fathers of the council promulgated four points: 1) the Son is God; what is said of God can be said of the Son; 2) the Son is the only begotten, not made; 3) the relationship between the

Father and the Son has no beginning and no end; and 4) the Father and the Son are *homooúsios* (hō-,mō-'ü-zē-us, *homo*="same"; *ousía*="essence", "being"), they are of one substance. In other words, to tell the story of the Son is to tell the story of God. We come to know God through the life of the Son, God in our midst. Soon after the council other formulae were composed and inserted into the Creed. In 381, the Council of Constantinople was called to settle on the final form of the Creed.

In the current translation of the Creed we proclaim that Jesus is "one in being" with the Father. You will note that the translators for the third edition use the word "consubstantial" to get closer to the original meaning of *homooúsios*. You might find that this is an uncommon word, not used in normal conversation, but the relationship between the Father and the Son is unique and therefore requires a special word. It took the early Church several centuries to define this unique relationship. You will also note that we no longer say that Jesus was "born of the Virgin" but rather "incarnate of the Virgin." This too more accurately describes the fullness of both natures of Jesus, divine and human, since the divine was present at his conception. To describe God's incarnation is more than simply being born as you and I were.

Praying the Nicene Creed

Leader: Let us pray the Nicene Creed together.

I believe in one God,
the Father almighty,
maker of heaven and earth,
of all things visible and invisible.

I believe in one Lord Jesus Christ,
the Only Begotten Son of God,
born of the Father before all ages.

God from God, Light from Light,
true God from true God,
begotten, not made, consubstantial with the Father;
through him all things were made.

For us men and for our salvation he came down from heaven,

At the words that follow, up to and including **and became man,** *all bow.*

and by the Holy Spirit was incarnate of the Virgin Mary,
and became man.

For our sake he was crucified under Pontius Pilate,
he suffered death and was buried,

and rose again on the third day
in accordance with the Scriptures.

He ascended into heaven
and is seated at the right hand of the Father.

He will come again in glory
to judge the living and the dead
and his kingdom will have no end.

I believe in the Holy Spirit, the Lord, the giver of life,
who proceeds from the Father and the Son,
who with the Father and the Son is adored and glorified,
who has spoken through the prophets.

I believe in one, holy, catholic and apostolic Church.

I confess one Baptism for the forgiveness of sins
and I look forward to the resurrection of the dead
and the life of the world to come. Amen.

Word of the Lord

Leader asks a participant to proclaim the Scripture passage.
John 20:24-29

Silent Reflection

What word, phrase, or image from the Scripture reading touches my heart or speaks to my life?
Reflect on this quietly or share it aloud.

Sharing Question

- Thomas said that he refused to believe Christ was risen until he could put his hands inside Jesus' actual wounds. What conditions do I place upon my own faith?

Reflection 2

Where Was Thomas?

So where was Thomas that first week when Jesus Christ first appeared? The Gospels never mention his whereabouts. We are not given even a glimpse as to why Thomas was not with the other Apostles. Where was he and what was he doing?

I gained new insight on a cross-country flight several years ago. Seated next to the window in the last row of the plane, I knew it was going to be a long flight so I had lots to read to prepare for a research paper I was about to write. As I nestled in and thanked God that the middle seat was still empty, the flight attendant announced that this was the only empty seat on the flight and the door was about to close. God is good! The Spirit was giving me an opportunity for peace and quiet so that I could read one of several books recommended by my bioethics professor. As I plunged into the book, I heard some commotion. I glanced up to find a middle-aged man huffing and puffing toward the last row. Fear and panic struck as this man, older and wider than I, approached the row that I had claimed as my sanctuary. I greeted him while I pushed my shoulder into the window as close as I could and buried my eyes into the pages of the book. Oh God, I prayed, please make him not be a talker.

Faith is not about seeing things or people with just our eyes. It means seeing beyond the surface of reality. Jesus invites us to come and see who he really is. And so it was on that flight. My row mate noticed the title of my book, *New Directions in Sexual Ethics: Moral Theology and the Challenge of AIDS*. His questions came in rapid succession. Halfway to Houston I was resigned to the reality that I would not be reading on this flight. My new friend quickly figured out that I was Catholic and must be involved in some sort of ministry. He began to tell his story.

"I was a Catholic," he said, "but I got divorced and you know what the church has to say about that, so I stopped going." Without hesitating he continued that he was flying from his retirement in Florida to Seattle to visit his son, who was now dying of AIDS. And of course, he added, "You must know what the Church thinks of my gay son. So, we are both pretty much outsiders." I felt his deep pain, and before I could even begin to speak I remembered the words of Paul: "You are no longer strangers and aliens … you also are built together spiritually into a dwelling place for God" (Ephesians 2:19-22).

Where was Thomas? He was on that flight. Both Thomas and my flight companion were in pain and alienated from the community. Thomas' absence in the Gospel story speaks volumes about the importance of each individual's

"In liturgical celebrations each person, minister or layman, who has an office to perform, should do all of, but only, those parts which pertain to his office by the nature of the rite and the principles of liturgy.

Servers, lectors, commentators, and members of the choir also exercise a genuine liturgical function. They ought, therefore, to discharge their office with the sincere piety and decorum demanded by so exalted a ministry and rightly expected of them by God's people.

Consequently they must all be deeply imbued with the spirit of the liturgy, each in his own measure, and they must be trained to perform their functions in a correct and orderly manner.

To promote active participation, the people should be encouraged to take part by means of acclamations, responses, psalmody, antiphons, and songs, as well as by actions, gestures, and bodily attitudes. And at the proper times all should observe a reverent silence."

—**Constitution on the Sacred Liturgy (Sacrosanctum Concilium),** **28-30**

participation with and in the gathered assembly. The God of mercy and goodness abounds within the community. Each one of us counts in God's reign and it is in and with the community, the people of God, where we find support to struggle with difficult times and broken spirits. It was the community who helped Thomas' discernment. The community is the home for all those not present.

Thomas' profession of faith is Christianity's ultimate truth, "My Lord and my God!" Thomas made his profession of faith in the presence of his companions. The community nurtured his faith to fullness in Christ. We are part of the whole body of Christ, and when one is missing or hurting we are all lost and hurt. The Gospel calls us to see beyond the surface to meet the real God.

> 66 *The God of mercy and goodness abounds within the community. Each one of us counts in God's reign and it is in and with the community, the people of God, where we find support to struggle with difficult times and broken spirits* 99

These stories are told to console us in times of pain and doubt and to encourage us to reach out to those who are marginalized and alienated. Thus, God keeps us close even when we are away. The Christian community is called to do nothing less when one of us hurts or is absent. Doubt and questioning can be necessary tools for the journey.

The goodness of God is that God reveals his self not just once, but again and again, and in new ways and at unexpected times. God continues to save us from ourselves. While we are all heirs of Christ's blessing, we are also descendants of Thomas. *Blessed are those who have not seen but have come to believe!* (John 20:29) And while we may not be able to see or to touch the wounds of the risen Christ, we are compelled by virtue of our transformation in Christ to see and to touch the wounds of the suffering and broken members of the body of Christ.

We need to have faith in Jesus Christ as individuals and must proclaim that belief as one Church. In the spirit of Thomas, the doubter and questioner, let us pray for the strength and the grace to keep showing up, to ask the right questions in the coming years so that our church may continue to say, "My Lord and my God," and to be a prophetic voice in the world. The enemy of faith is not doubt but a smug and self-satisfied certainty.

Invitation to Share

- Was there a time when I felt like an outsider?

- How have my struggles, and even doubts, led me to deeper faith?

- Who in my life has helped me to grow in faith? Share how someone has played a role in your faith journey.

Missioning

Determine a specific action (individual or group) that flows from your sharing. This should be your primary consideration for choosing an action. If choosing an individual action, determine what you will do and share it with the group. If choosing a group action, determine who will take responsibility for different aspects of the action.

The following are secondary suggestions:

- Prepare for next Sunday's liturgy by prayerfully reading and reflecting on the Scripture readings during the week. The readings can be found on the U.S. Conference of Catholic Bishops' website, www.usccb.org/nab/

- Find out how your parish or diocese ministers to outsiders—for example, persons with AIDS, immigrants, inactive Catholics, young adults, etc.—and volunteer to help.

Sending Forth

Leader: Let us close this session by renewing our baptismal promises.

Pause, until each member has a lighted candle.

Leader: Do you reaffirm your renunciation of evil
and renew your commitment to Jesus Christ?

All: I do.

Leader: Do you believe in God the Father?

**All: I believe in God, the Father almighty,
creator of heaven and earth.**

Leader: Do you believe in Jesus Christ, the Son of God?

**All: I believe in Jesus Christ, his only Son, our Lord.
He was conceived by the power of the Holy Spirit
and born of the Virgin Mary.
He suffered under Pontius Pilate,
was crucified, died and was buried.
He descended to the dead.
On the third day he rose again.
He ascended into heaven,
and is seated at the right hand of the Father.
He will come again to judge
the living and the dead.**

> Leader: Do you believe in the Holy Spirit?
>
> **All:** **I believe in the Holy Spirit,**
> **the holy catholic Church,**
> **the communion of saints,**
> **the forgiveness of sins,**
> **the resurrection of the body,**
> **and life everlasting.**
>
> Leader: May Almighty God,
> the Father of Our Lord Jesus Christ,
> who has given us a new birth by water
> and the Holy Spirit,
> and bestowed upon us the forgiveness of sins,
> keep us in eternal life by his grace,
> in Christ Jesus our Lord.
>
> **All:** **Amen.**

Conclude with the Our Father, the Sign of Peace, and the closing song.

Sign of Peace

> Leader: The peace of the Lord be with you always.
> **Response:** **And with your spirit.**

Song Suggestion

 "Have Faith, Believe in Me," Paule Freeburg, D.C., Christopher Walker (OCP) *See Appendix for lyrics.*

Next Steps

Prepare for your next session by prayerfully reading and studying:

- Session Five: "Until You Come Again"

- Mark 8:1-21

- Eucharistic Prayer II, paying special attention to the wording in the institution narratives. You can find the text on the U.S. Conference of Catholic Bishops' website, http://www.usccb.org/romanmissal/samples-priest-prayer2.shtm

Session Five

UNTIL YOU COME AGAIN

Suggested Environment

A Bible, a candle, and other appropriate objects, such as a missalette or the pew card that accompanies Lifting Up Our Hearts, *may be arranged on a small table.*

Invitation to Pray

Leader: Let us put ourselves in the presence of the Lord.

The group gives itself over to several moments of deepening silence as each member pays attention to her or his breathing, and slowly prays for stillness.

Leader: In the name of the Father, the Son and the Holy Spirit.

Pray together: **We stand before you, Holy Spirit,**
conscious of our sinfulness,
but aware that we gather in your name.

Come to us, remain with us,
and enlighten our hearts.

Give us light and strength
to know your will,
to make it our own,
and to live it in our lives.

Guide us by your wisdom,
support us by your power,
for you are God,
sharing the glory of Father and Son.

You desire justice for all:
enable us to uphold the rights of others;
do not allow us to be misled by ignorance
or corrupted by fear or favor.

"Although the sacred liturgy is above all things the worship of the divine Majesty, it likewise contains much instruction for the faithful. For in the liturgy God speaks to His people and Christ is still proclaiming His gospel. And the people reply to God both by song and prayer. Moreover, the prayers addressed to God by the priest who presides over the assembly in the person of Christ are said in the name of the entire holy people and of all present. And the visible signs used by the liturgy to signify invisible divine things have been chosen by Christ or the Church. Thus not only when things are read 'which were written for our instruction' (*Romans 15:4*), but also when the Church prays or sings or acts, the faith of those taking part is nourished and their minds are raised to God, so that they may offer Him their rational service and more abundantly receive His grace."

—Constitution on the Sacred Liturgy (Sacrosanctum Concilium), 33

Unite us to yourself in the bond of love
and keep us faithful to all that is true.

As we gather in your name
may we temper justice with love,
so that all our decisions
may be pleasing to you,
and earn the reward
promised to good and faithful servants.
Amen.

(This prayer was said before every session of Vatican II)

Song Suggestion

 "Your Words Are Spirit and Life," by Bernadette Farrell (OCP). *See Appendix for lyrics.*

Living Our Faith

Share briefly your experience of putting into effect the action you chose after the last session.

Reflection 1

Words Matter

Words do matter. Pseudo-Dionysius, considered to be the first liturgical theologian and one of the most influential mystical writers of the ancient church, lived during the late fifth and early sixth centuries. His writings describe the experience of the Divine Liturgy as a place where the sacred mysteries are taught to the initiated. He wrote that while God is beyond all names, the liturgy teaches through actions, signs, symbols, and words. It is through our liturgical celebrations that the formless and unutterable are given form and expression.

Let's look at some of the words of the prayers in the *Third Edition of the Roman Missal* that we will pray later in this session. In the Invitation to Prayer, we ask God to accept the gifts brought forth: fruits of the earth and work of human hands for the glory of God's name, for our own good and the good of the whole Church, which is holy. This addition of the word "holy" is an important recognition of the status of God's people in the church. The gifts are holy because they are the fruit of the Creator and the work of human hands. The Lord hears the prayer and accepts the sacrifice, and the Church benefits from the prayer. Publicly proclaimed prayer develops a collective and cooperative consciousness that flows from the community's memory.

Eucharist is about fulfilling Christ's command. As our new response to the Preface declares, "It is right and just." Our response reclaims our birthright for justice. In baptism we witness a God who is both present and yet to come. If baptism makes us members of the body of Christ (*ecclesia*) and Christ is the source of communion (*koinonia*), then the Eucharist makes the Church. Baptism seals us into the one body of "the new covenant" through the death and resurrection of Jesus. Faith should connect us to the past as it helps us live the present, which energizes us for the future.

In the "Holy, Holy, Holy," we will say or sing "Lord God of Hosts" rather than "God of power and might." "Hosts" refers to God's command over a choir of angels while conveying the idea of God's power over heaven and earth. It means the invisible powers that work at God's command. The new edition of the *Roman Missal* emphasizes the transcendent power of God.

The Memorial Acclamations use the call and response format. The priest says, "The mystery of faith," and we respond with a prayer proclaiming the Paschal Mystery. This proclamation is the core of our faith, it is who we are as Christians. Most notable among the new acclamations is the absence of the familiar response: "Christ has died, Christ is risen, Christ will come again." This proclamation does not follow the form and rhythm of the other prayer responses; it was merely a statement of faith, although well used and loved. The new eucharistic acclamations include us ("*We* proclaim" and "When *we* eat" and "Save *us*") and speak of what Christ did for us ("*you* have set *us* free").

Responding to the Invitation to Prayer

Leader: Let us pray the "Invitation to Prayer."

Leader: Pray my sisters and brothers.
**Response: May the Lord accept the sacrifice at your hands
for the praise and glory of his name,
for our good and the good of all his holy Church.**

Praying the Preface Dialogue

Leader: Let us pray the Preface Dialogue.

Leader: The Lord be with you.
Response: And with your spirit.

"God who 'wills that all be saved and come to the knowledge of the truth' [*1 Timothy 2:4*], 'who in many and various ways spoke in times past to the fathers by the prophets' [*Hebrews 1:1*]. When the fullness of time had come sent his Son, the Word made flesh, anointed by the Holy Spirit, to preach the Gospel to the poor, to heal the contrite of heart; he is 'the physician, being both flesh and of the Spirit,' the mediator between God and us. For his humanity, united with the person of the Word, was the instrument of our salvation. Therefore in Christ, 'the perfect achievement of our reconciliation came forth and the fullness of divine worship was given to us'."

—Constitution on the Sacred Liturgy (*Sacrosanctum Concilium*), 5

Leader: Lift up your hearts.
Response: We lift them up to the Lord.

Leader: Let us give thanks to the Lord our God.
Response: It is right and just.

Praying the Preface Acclamation (Holy, Holy, Holy)

Leader: Let us pray the "Preface Acclamation."

**Holy, Holy, Holy Lord God of hosts.
Heaven and earth are full of your glory.
Hosanna in the highest.
Blessed is he who comes
in the name of the Lord.
Hosanna in the highest.**

Alternatively, the Preface Acclamation may be sung.

10 "Holy," from the revised *Mass of Glory* by Ken Canedo and Bob Hurd (OCP). *See Appendix for lyrics.*

Praying the Mystery of Faith (Memorial Acclamations)

Leader: Let us pray each of the Memorial Acclamations.

Leader: The mystery of faith.
**Response: We proclaim your Death, O Lord,
and profess your Resurrection
until you come again.**

Leader: The mystery of faith:
**Response: When we eat this Bread and drink this Cup,
we proclaim your Death, O Lord,
until you come again.**

Leader: The mystery of faith:
**Response: Save us, Savior of the world,
for by your Cross and Resurrection
you have set us free.**

Word of the Lord

Leader asks a participant to proclaim the Scripture passage.
Mark 8:1-21

Silent Reflection

What word, phrase, or image from the Scripture reading touches my heart or speaks to my life? Reflect on this quietly or share it aloud.

Sharing Question

- At what times do I feel that I do not have enough or only half a loaf?

- What would the world look like if we really lived in hope and anticipation of the kingdom of God? What would my life look like?

Reflection 2

Eucharist Is a Verb

This Gospel story, one of my favorites, reminds me of my youth in Chicago. Most of my Catholic friends dreaded Fridays because of fish sticks. I, however, relished Fridays since my Dad would always bring home some fresh smelt and sauté them. I never had a fish stick until high school, where they were a major portion of the Lenten cafeteria menu. I had always imagined that the miracle of this story was about all the folks having plenty of smelt to eat and cooked in my Dad's style. When I moved to the west coast, I was disappointed to discover that smelt were not to be found other than in bait and tackle shops.

Imagine my joy when I inadvertently discovered fresh smelt in a Puget Sound fish store. The sign advertised "Fresh Smelt" so I ran into the small but very crowded shop, took a number, and waited my turn. As a very robust female voice called my number, I jostled my way to the counter and boldly proclaimed "Some smelts, please!" To which she answered in disdain: "The plural of smelt is still smelt and we are out of 'em." Rather sobering in front of the crowd in that store.

When I ask my little godchildren what they enjoy most about going to Mass, the answer is usually "Getting to talk to my friends." Children already know at an early age that the theology of story is also about relationship. This is not only a comforting message to today's individualistic world but also an invitation to share in relationship with each other and thereby possibly with our God.

Can you imagine four thousand people sitting down to share a meal, no matter how simple it was, without talking, without sharing a story or two, perhaps, even sharing their own stories? In this Gospel story, the people were fed on bread and story. They were filled because they were given a time and a space to share their stories as they did the bread. This Gospel story is about building community. This is a story about our generous God who calls us to abundance. It is about a very hospitable and compassionate Jesus, who really cares about us. Mark proclaims that those who are hungry will have enough to eat. There is enough to share and never to be exhausted. Christ is always with us as we wait in hope for his return. We share ourselves by listening to others' journeys of life, especially their conflicts and doubts. We hold and cherish in those journeys the presence of *Emmanuel*—God with us. Then by sharing our own journey we at the same time share the faith that helps us to make sense of, or deal with the ups and downs, the questions and complexities of life in our society. For Mark, story is very important because it is all about faith. Our story is a window into our faith as well as a mirror for our faith, through which we come to know God in our own lives.

> **❝** *Can you imagine four thousand people sitting down to share a meal, no matter how simple it was, without talking, without sharing a story or two, perhaps, even sharing their own stories?* **❞**

We proclaim in our liturgies the model of the reign of God and ritually express our longing for the "promised future," as does Mark's Gospel. Liturgy sustains and nourishes us in our ministries as disciples of Christ. The worshipping assembly, as did the four thousand, transcends our individuality and emphasizes our communal identity. We gather because we are called, like the multitudes, and because we are obeying Jesus' command to give thanks and share word and bread in his remembrance until his return. Eucharist, from the Greek verb *eucharistia*, is the act of giving thanks in community. So the basic nature of Eucharist is relationship to God and to each other. The gift giver becomes the gift broken and poured out. This is what Christ does at the Eucharist and it is what we are missioned and sent forth from each eucharistic celebration to share with the world.

The Second Vatican Council reminded us that the Eucharist is the source and summit of Christian life, which was reaffirmed in the recent Synod of Bishops on the Eucharist who wrote of the "beneficial influence that the liturgical reform implemented since the Second Vatican Council has had for the life of the Church." We must recapture a notion of Eucharist as action instead of passive reception. Eucharist is thanksgiving for our share of divine life through Christ. Eucharist is about sharing. Eucharist is about the gift-giver becoming the gift. Christ shares himself and is the gift-giver broken, shared, and poured out. As members of the body of Christ we are sent forth to be Eucharist for the world. According to Pope John Paul II, "Whoever receives Christ in the reality of his body and blood cannot keep this gift to himself, but is impelled to share it in courageous witness of the Gospel, in service to brothers in difficulty, in forgiveness for offenses."

"Become what you receive: the Body of Christ, given for the world."

—St. Augustine

Invitation to Share

- How am I Eucharist to other people?

- How can I be an active rather than passive participant in the Eucharistic Prayer?

Missioning

Determine a specific action (individual or group) that flows from your sharing. This should be your primary consideration for choosing an action. If choosing an individual action, determine what you will do and share it with the group. If choosing a group action, determine who will take responsibility for different aspects of the action.

The following are secondary suggestions:

- Prepare for next Sunday's liturgy by prayerfully reading and reflecting on the Scripture readings during the week.

- Find the Eucharistic Prayers online (www.usccb.org/romanmissal). Select one Eucharistic Prayer to read and contemplate as part of your preparation for Sunday Mass. How does the Eucharistic Prayer connect with your own story? How does this story continue through the life of your community? Consider journaling your responses.

- During the week, journal about the ways that liturgy and your daily life are consistent or how they could be more consistent.

Sending Forth

The leader invites the people to think about all they have heard and experienced during the session.

> Leader: As we come to our closing prayer, for whom do we pray,
> and what do we pray for this night?

Participants offer individual petitions and all respond, "Until You Come Again."

Conclude with the Our Father, the Sign of Peace, and the closing song.

Sign of Peace

> Leader: The peace of the Lord be with you always.
> **Response: And with your spirit.**

Song Suggestion

11   "We Are Called to Serve, We Are Called by Grace," Tim Smith, Julie Smith (OCP) *See Appendix for lyrics.*

Next Steps

Prepare for your next session by prayerfully reading and studying:

- Session Six: "I Shall Be Healed to Go Forth"

- Luke 7:1-10

- For additional scriptural references see Matthew 8:5-13; Rev 19:9; cf John 1:29, 36; Rev. 5:6-13; 22:1-3.

Session Six

I SHALL BE HEALED TO GO FORTH

Suggested Environment

A Bible, a candle, and other appropriate objects, such as a missalette or the pew card that accompanies Lifting Up Our Hearts, *may be arranged on a small table.*

Invitation to Pray

    Leader: Let us put ourselves in the presence of the Lord.

The group gives itself over to several moments of deepening silence as each member pays attention to her or his breathing, and slowly prays for stillness.

    Leader: In the name of the Father, the Son and the Holy Spirit.

Pray together: **We stand before you, Holy Spirit,
conscious of our sinfulness,
but aware that we gather in your name.**

                **Come to us, remain with us,
and enlighten our hearts.**

                **Give us light and strength
to know your will,
to make it our own,
and to live it in our lives.**

                **Guide us by your wisdom,
support us by your power,
for you are God,
sharing the glory of Father and Son.**

                **You desire justice for all:
enable us to uphold the rights of others;
do not allow us to be misled by ignorance
or corrupted by fear or favor.**

> **Unite us to yourself in the bond of love**
> **and keep us faithful to all that is true.**
>
> **As we gather in your name**
> **may we temper justice with love,**
> **so that all our decisions**
> **may be pleasing to you,**
> **and earn the reward**
> **promised to good and faithful servants.**
> **Amen.**
>
> *(This prayer was said before every session of Vatican II)*

Song Suggestion

 "I Say 'Yes,' Lord / Digo 'Sí,' Señor," Donna Peña (GIA)
See Appendix for lyrics.

Living Our Faith

Share briefly your experience of putting into effect the action you chose after the last session.

Reflection 1

Openness to the Gospel

Mark Twain once wrote, "It ain't the parts of the Bible I don't understand that bother me, it's the parts I do understand." There is a bit of Mark Twain in all of us, especially when the words of the Gospel cause us discomfort. What are we to make of some of the things Jesus says? What about other characters who say and do things we least expect?

In the new "Invitation to Communion," the priest prays, "Behold the Lamb of God, behold him who takes away the sins of the world. Blessed are those called to the supper of the Lamb." When we respond, "Lord, I am not worthy that you should enter under my roof, but only say the word and my soul shall be healed," we echo the words of the Roman centurion who begged Jesus to heal his servant. Although Jews were prohibited from entering the homes of non-Jews, Jesus entered the centurion's home and healed his servant. Remarkably it will be the words of the centurion we will recite before we receive the body and blood of Christ. It clearly is a statement of faith by a Gentile, one who was on the outside, and yet we will all say those same words as insiders.

The implications of the Gospel are not only bothersome but downright staggering. If Christians took Jesus at his word, the history of the world would be vastly different. How are we to make sense of the Gospel and to live its message in the twenty-first century? Do we not sometimes find ourselves rationalizing that it is not practical in today's world, and that Jesus is only giving us an ideal?

We must stay open to the possibility that the Gospel will rise up at some future date to confront us where we live. Taking Jesus at his word calls for an openness, which is far more demanding than laws and virtues. It is relatively easy to set a standard of behavior and keep to it, such as writing an annual check to your favorite charity. It is much more difficult to be open to the kind of God who can call us to different actions in different situations at different times.

> *How are we to make sense of the Gospel and to live its message in the twenty-first century?*

Why does God call for such openness? It preserves our dependence on God and it keeps us simple. Our initial commitment to Christ is not enough because nothing human is absolute or final. Every day, our lives increase or diminish. Openness keeps us focused on the basics: What is God asking of me? What stands in the way of my allowing Jesus to come under my roof?

The Gospel is always speaking to us in new ways. Jesus assures us that we are not alone; with God all things are possible. That is what we do in our liturgies. We listen to God's Word and through that listening we take a posture of openness in our prayer. This moves us to our humble acceptance as we say "Amen" to our brokenness in Christ's body broken and shared and Christ's blood poured out for us. It is here that we are united with all those who have said "Amen" before us, those who now proclaim "Amen" with us, and those who are yet to exclaim "Amen."

God will be with us as we take all that we have received and move from this place to share in new ways and in different times what we have received. Our "Amen" is not the end, it is just the beginning!

Responding to the Invitation to Communion

Leader: Let us pray the "Invitation to Communion."

Leader: Behold the Lamb of God,
behold him who takes away the sins of the world.
Blessed are those called to the supper of the Lamb.

Response: **Lord, I am not worthy**
that you should enter under my roof,
but only say the word
and my soul shall be healed.

"The Church ... earnestly desires that Christ's faithful, when present at this mystery of faith, should not be there as strangers or silent spectators; on the contrary, through a good understanding of the rites and prayers they should take part in the sacred service conscious of what they are doing, with devotion and full involvement. They should be instructed by God's word and be nourished at the table of the Lord's body; they should give thanks to God; by offering the Immaculate Victim, not only through the hands of the priest but also with him, they should learn to offer themselves as well; through Christ the Mediator, they should be formed day by day into an ever more perfect unity with God and with each other, so that finally God may be all in all."

—*Sacrosanctum Concilium*, 48

Word of the Lord

Leader asks a participant to proclaim the Scripture passage.
Luke 7:1-10

Silent Reflection

What word, phrase, or image from the Scripture reading touches my heart or speaks to my life?
Reflect on this quietly or share it aloud.

Sharing Question

- How do I welcome Christ in my life? What stands in the way of my inviting Jesus to come under my roof?

Reflection 2

Go Forth

A good friend of mine called not so long ago and asked if a frozen turkey would still be good after a year in the freezer. I offered that it probably would not be harmful, if it were thawed in the refrigerator and cooked properly, although it was well beyond what the Food and Drug Administration would advise. But I did add that it probably wouldn't taste very good either. To that my dear friend replied, "Well, then I'll just give it to the food bank."

That's a pretty good story about bad giving. It's the kind of giving that looks like giving but really isn't. You know the kind I mean—giving the old clothes and worn out shoes and socks to Goodwill or to the St. Vincent DePaul Society. It is the giving that gives nothing away that is essential or good or valuable. God gave to us in a very different way—not the freezer-burned turkey but the very best, Jesus Christ.

God gives us from the center of his self, from the core of the divine treasury, God's only Son: Jesus Christ. God gives from a full heart and abundant spirit. And what God gives us in Jesus Christ is forgiveness, freedom, and healing. We come to receive that precious gift every time we are invited to approach the table of the Lord.

Jesus Christ gave his life so that we might have life. We are blessed as the priest proclaims, "Behold the Lamb of God, behold him who takes away the sins of the world. Blessed are those called to the supper of the Lamb." God does desire to live within us and among us, but God does not barge into our midst. We express our unworthiness and acknowledge our faith in this wonderful mystery of an incarnational God who desires to live under our roof when we say: "Lord, I am not worthy that you should enter under my roof, but only say the word and my soul shall be healed."

Healing because we are forgiven and freed does not take us back in time. It does not undo what we have done badly or spoken wrongly. It does not undo the hurtful things that have been done to us. Healing transforms us into new selves personally and communally in the image and likeness of Christ. For God so loved the world that God gave his only Son, so that everyone who believes in him may not perish but may have eternal life.

Eternal life—wow! God's grace gathers us in and then sends us forth. We gather to scatter! God didn't give us the old frozen turkey or worn-out clothes. God gave us his beloved son, Jesus, and Jesus, like his father, gave from the very core of his being. Jesus Christ offers us pardon and gives us the Church so that we can be forgiven, healed and become what we eat. We come to the table to experience once again how God gives to us and how Jesus lives with us in freedom from sin. Together the Father and the Son proved the truth promised: You can have what you give away. We become what we eat.

> ❝ *God gave us his beloved son, Jesus, and Jesus, like his father, gave from the very core of his being* ❞

The opposite truth is that we cannot have what we hold on to; we can have only what we give away. That is what God's invitation to forgiveness brings us: freedom. Freedom does not come from a freezer or from the back of God's closet. Freedom lets us turn toward the light so that we can bask in the warmth of God's abundant grace and life.

This freedom creates a community of forgiving sojourners. Here we come as a community to be forgiven and freed. Sin deceived us into thinking we could have it all only if we grabbed it for ourselves. But as a community we seek forgiveness and healing. God will give to us once again from God's treasure, freely and in abundance. God's gift is always much more than we ask. God will bond us into a community of forgiven and forgiving people. Together, we are then freed to be the body of Christ. Through this infusion of divine love, God gives each of us the power of all of us, united in love in the Triune Spirit of God.

What an adventure awaits us. God's people, broken and healed: the Church. At God's hand we journey with Christ freed and sent forth to glorify the Lord by our transformed lives, to go forth and announce the Gospel. Our story is the Paschal Mystery, which we celebrate anew in every Eucharist.

Invitation to Share

- How does our parish community live the Eucharist?

- In the Scripture passage Jesus recognized the centurion as a model of faith. How has someone been a model of faith for me?

- How can I be a healing presence to others?

- How do I live during the week what we celebrate on Sunday?

Missioning

Determine a specific action (individual or group) that flows from your sharing. This should be your primary consideration for choosing an action. If choosing an individual action, determine what you will do and share it with the group. If choosing a group action, determine who will take responsibility for different aspects of the action.

The following are secondary suggestions:

- Prepare for next Sunday's liturgy by prayerfully reading and reflecting on the Scripture readings during the week.

- Invite others to study the *Third Edition of the Roman Missal* with you.

- Find out what your parish does to reach out to people in need, and get involved.

Sending Forth

The leader invites the people to think about all they have heard and experienced during the session.

> Leader: As we come to our closing prayer, for whom do we pray, and what do we pray for this night?

Participants offer individual petitions and all respond, "I shall be healed to go forth."

Conclude with the Our Father, the Sign of Peace, and the closing song.

Sign of Peace

> Leader: The peace of the Lord be with you always.
> **Response: And with your spirit.**

Song Suggestion

13 "How Can We Not But Sing," Donna Peña (GIA)
See Appendix for lyrics.

Praying the Concluding Rite

Leader: You may hear the following when a bishop is the celebrant.

Leader: Let us pray the "Concluding Rite."

Leader: Blessed be the name of the Lord.
Response: Now and for ever.

Leader: Our help is in the name of the Lord.
Response: Who made heaven and earth.

Leader: May almighty God bless us, ✠ the Father, the Son, and the Holy Spirit.
Response: Amen.

Leader: Go forth and announce the Gospel of the Lord.
Response: Thanks be to God.

Leader: Go in peace, glorifying the Lord by your life.
Response: Thanks be to God.

Leader: Go in peace.
Response: Thanks be to God.

Next Steps

After completing *Lifting Up Our Hearts: Praying the Third Edition of the Roman Missal*, continue meeting to faith share. Consider using the edition of *PrayerTime: Faith-Sharing Reflections on the Sunday Gospels* that matches the liturgical year (**visit www.renewintl.org**).

Music Resources

Most of the songs suggested for the sessions can be found in the standard hymnals or parish worship aids. Should you want to get in touch with any of the publishers of the songs suggested (for example, to obtain printed copies of the music scores, or to purchase downloadable PDF, TIFF, or MP3 files, or to ask for permission to reprint copyright words), here are their contact details.

GIA Publications, Inc.
7404 South Mason Avenue
Chicago, IL 60638
Phone: 800-442-1358 or
708-496-3800
Website: www.giamusic.com
Email: custserv@giamusic.com

Oregon Catholic Press Publications (OCP)
5536 NE Hassalo
Portland, OR 97213
Phone: 800-LITURGY (548-8749)
Website: www.ocp.org
Email: liturgy@ocp.org

World Library Publications
3708 River Road, Suite 400
Franklin Park, IL 60131
Phone: 800-566-6150
Website: www.wlpmusic.com

Order the companion music CD.

Visit our website
www.renewintl.org/missal

Alphabetical Index of Suggested Songs

Be Merciful, O Lord / Misericordia
Words: based on Psalm 51 © ICEL and Conferencia Episcopal Española. Music: © World Library Publications.

Glory to God (from the revised Mass of Glory)
Words © ICEL. Music: Ken Canedo and Bob Hurd. © OCP Publications.

Have Faith, Believe in Me
Words and music: Paule Freeburg, DC and Christopher Walker. © OCP Publications.

Holy (from the revised Mass of Glory)
Words © ICEL. Music: Ken Canedo and Bob Hurd. © OCP Publications.

How Can We Not Sing?
Words and music: Donna Peña. © 1992 GIA Publications, Inc.

I Say "Yes," Lord / Digo "Sí," Señor
Words and music: Donna Peña. © 1989 GIA Publications, Inc.

If You Believe and I Believe
Words: traditional Zimbabwean. Music: Zimbabwean melody adaptation of traditional English melody. Published by OCP Publications.

Lord Show Us Your Mercy and Love
Words: based on Psalm 85:9-10a, 10b-11, 13-14. Refrain text: ©1969, 1981, 1997 ICEL. All rights reserved. Music and verses text: Janet Sullivan Whitaker. © 2004 Janet Sullivan Whitaker. Published by OCP Publications.

Send Us Your Spirit
Words and music: Daniel L. Schutte. ©1985 Daniel L. Schutte. Published by OCP Publications.

Send Out Your Spirit
Words: based on Psalm 104. Words and music: Jesse Manibusan. © 1996, 1997 Jesse Manibusan. Published by Spiritandsong.com.

We Are Called to Serve, We Are Called by Grace
Words and music: Tim Smith and Julie Smith. © 1990 OCP Publications.

You Alone
Words and music: Sarah Hart and Dwight Liles. © OCP Publications.

Your Words are Spirit and Life
Words: based on Psalm 19: 8-11 and music: Bernadette Farrell © 1992 Bernadette Farrell. Published by OCP Publications.

Lyrics: Session One

Opening Song
SEND US YOUR SPIRIT
Dan Schutte

1 Send us your Spirit, O Lord.
Evening enfolds us
And holds us too near.
Wake the morning light.
Make our living bright.
Shine on our darkness, O Lord.

2 Teach us your wisdom, O Lord.
Shadows have clouded,
have crowded our sight.
Give us hearts that see.
Set our loving free.
Hear us and help us, O Lord.

3 Send us good summer, O Lord.
Winters have chilled us,
and stilled us too long.
Give us love's own fire.
Be our true desire.
Send us your Spirit, O Lord.

Closing Song
SEND OUT YOUR SPIRIT
(PSALM 104)
Jesse Manibusan

REFRAIN
O God, send out your Spirit;
renew the face of the earth.
O God, send out your Spirit;
renew the face of the earth.

1 We bless you, O God,
for you are so great.
Your Spirit uncovers
hidden beauty and grace.

Though times we deny
all the pain and the tears,
your Spirit empowers us
and soon we face our fear.

2 Every prayer we pray,
sacred word, sacred rite,
is for the ones who are left waiting outside.
Ev'ry sermon we preach,
ev'ry Spirit-filled tune;
Love says, "Remember why we
do the things we do."

3 Every time a person reaching out
is turned away by the racist
prejudicial attitudes of hate,
we are called to break the silence,
sanctioning the shame,
stepping across the lines of this
sometimes unholy game.

4 Sources of oppression
that we haven't really faced;
human inhumanity upon
the human race.
Spirit ever faithful,
Spirit ever true,
rain down all around,
and every heart renew.

Lyrics: Session Two

Opening Song
BE MERCIFUL O LORD

REFRAIN
Be merciful, O Lord, for we have sinned.
Misericordia, Señor, hemos pecado.
Be merciful, O Lord, for we have sinned.
Misericordia, Señor, hemos pecado.

1 Dios mío por tu bondad, misericordia
Por tu inmensa compasión borra mi culpa
Lávame de todos mis delitos
y limpia mi pecado

2 For I acknowledge well my offense,
And my sin is always before me.
Against you only have I sinned,
And done what is evil in your sight.

3 O Dios crea en mi un corazón puro
Renuevame un espíritu firme
No me arrojes lejos de tu rostro
Ni tu Santo Espíritu me quites

4 Give me back the joy of your salvation,
A willing spirit sustain in me.
Lord, open my lips and my mouth shall
proclaim your praise.

Closing Song
LORD, SHOW US YOUR MERCY AND LOVE
Janet Sullivan Whitaker

REFRAIN
Lord show us your mercy and love.
Show us your mercy, show us your love.
Lord show us your mercy and love.
Show us your mercy, show us your love.

1 I will hear what you proclaim:
words of peace for all.
Show us your mercy, show us your love.
You are always near
to those who seek salvation.
Show us your mercy, show us your love.

2 How your glory fills the earth,
flowing through our land!
Show us your mercy, show us your love.
Kindness and truth shall meet,
peace and justice kiss.
Show us your mercy, show us your love.

3 Fountains of truth shall spring up
fresh from the earth.
Show us your mercy, show us your love.
Justice shall smile upon the earth
from up in heaven.
Show us your mercy, show us your love.

4 You provide everything we need.
Oh, you provide a land that gives us food.
Holy God, let justice walk before you,
and peace will light the way.

Lyrics: Session Three

Opening Song
YOU ALONE
Sarah Hart and Dwight Liles

REFRAIN
You alone are holy, you alone are Lord.
You alone are worthy to be honored
and adored.
Mercy you have given, kindness you
have shown.
Love is you alone.

1 Who of us is sinless in this place?
Who of us deserves your saving grace?
Who of us is good at all without your
blessed love
that falls upon our hearts to heal
our brokenness?

2 What is there to do but thank you, then,
for the gift that we might call you friend?
Greater love has not been known than
that for which you gave
your only son, that you might see us,
pure and blessed.

Words and music: Sarah Hart and Dwight Liles.
© OCP Publications. All rights reserved.

Closing Song
GLORY TO GOD
FROM THE REVISED
MASS OF GLORY

REFRAIN
Glory to God, glory to God,
glory to God in the highest,
and on earth peace to people of good will.
Glory to God, glory to God,
glory to God in the highest,
and on earth peace to people of good will.

1 We praise you, we bless you,
we adore you, we glorify you,
we give you thanks for your great glory,
Lord God, heavenly King,
O God, almighty Father.

Glory to God, glory to God,
glory to God in the highest,
and on earth peace to people of good will.

2 Lord Jesus Christ, Only Begotten Son,
Lord God, Lamb of God,
Son of the Father,
you take away the sins of the world,
have mercy on us;
you take away the sins of the world,
receive our prayer;
you are seated at the right hand
of the Father,
have mercy on us.

Glory to God, glory to God,
glory to God in the highest,
and on earth peace to people of good will.

3 For you alone are the Holy One,
you alone are the Lord,
you alone are the Most High, Jesus Christ,
with the Holy Spirit,
in the glory of God the Father.

Glory to God, glory to God,
glory to God in the highest,
and on earth peace to people of good will.
Glory to God, glory to God,
glory to God in the highest,
and on earth peace to people of good will.

Amen. Amen. Amen.

Words © ICEL Music: Ken Canedo and Bob
Hurd. All rights reserved. © OCP Publications.
All rights reserved.

Lyrics: Session Four

Opening Song
IF YOU BELIEVE AND I BELIEVE

If you believe and I believe
and we together pray,
the Holy Spirit must come down
and set God's people free,
and set God's people free,
and set God's people free;
the Holy Spirit must come down
and set God's people free.

Words: traditional Zimbabwean. Music: Zimbabwean melody adaptation of traditional English melody. Published by OCP Publications. All rights reserved.

Closing Song
HAVE FAITH; BELIEVE IN ME
Paule Freeburg, DC and Christopher Walker

Have faith, believe in me.
Have faith, believe in me.
I'm here for you.

Have faith, believe in me.
Have faith, believe in me.
I'm here for you.
Believe!

1 Jesus, you're so good to us.
   every day so good to us.

Have faith, believe in me.
Have faith, believe in me.
I'm here for you.
Have faith, believe in me.
Have faith, believe in me.
I'm here for you.
Believe!

2 You fill us with your love and light,
   live in us as love and light.

Have faith, believe in me.
Have faith, believe in me.
I'm here for you.
Have faith, believe in me.
Have faith, believe in me.
I'm here for you.
Believe!

3 We praise you, Jesus, every day,
   praise and thank you every day.

Have faith, believe in me.
Have faith, believe in me.
I'm here for you.
Have faith, believe in me.
Have faith, believe in me.
I'm here for you.
Believe!

Words and music: Paule Freeburg, DC and Christopher Walker. © OCP Publications. All rights reserved.

Lyrics: Session Five

Opening Song
YOUR WORDS ARE SPIRIT AND LIFE (Psalm 19)
Bernadette Farrell

Refrain
Your words are spirit and life O, Lord:
richer than gold, stronger than death.
Your words are spirit and life O, Lord;
life everlasting.

1 God's law is perfect, refreshing the soul,
reviving the weary spirit.
God's rule can be trusted: bringing us
wisdom, bringing God's wisdom to birth.

2 God's precepts keep us; their purpose
is right.
They gladden the hearts of people.
God's command is so clear it brings us
new vision;
bringing God's light to our eyes.

3 Living by God's truth is holy and sure;
God's presence is everlasting.
God's truth is eternal, bringing us justice;
bringing God's justice to earth.

4 God's word is precious, desired more
than gold;
worth more than we dare imagine and,
sweeter than honey, this word will feed us,
bringing fulfillment and joy.

Words based on Psalm 19: 8-11, Words and music © 1992 Bernadette Farrell. Published by OCP Publications. All rights reserved.

Optional Song
HOLY
FROM THE REVISED
MASS OF GLORY

Refrain
Holy, Holy, Holy Lord God of hosts.
Heaven and earth are full of your glory.
Hosanna, hosanna, hosanna in the highest.
Blessed is he who comes in the
name of the Lord.
Hosanna, hosanna, hosanna in the highest.

Words © ICEL. Music: Ken Canedo and Bob Hurd. © OCP Publications. All rights reserved.

Closing Song
WE ARE CALLED TO SERVE, WE ARE CALLED BY GRACE
Tim Smith and Julie Smith

Refrain
We are called to serve,
we are called by grace
to cherish Christ in every face.
We are call to serve,
we are called by name,
and in all we are,
God's love proclaim.

1 Called beyond our human understanding,
called before the world came into view.
Within your mother's womb,
your name was known to me
for you did not choose me, no, I chose you.

2 Called to be a light amid the darkness,
called to help a doubting world believe.
"Empowered by my Spirit,
anointed with my love,
you are called to give and share what you
believe."

Words and music: Tim Smith and Julie Smith. © 1990 OCP Publications All rights reserved.

Lyrics: Session Six

Opening Song
I SAY "YES," LORD /
DIGO "SÍ," SEÑOR
Donna Peña

1 To the God who can not die:
I say "Yes," my Lord.
I say "Yes," my Lord.
To the One who hears me cry:
I say "Yes," my Lord.
I say "Yes," my Lord.
To the God of the oppressed:
I say "Yes," my Lord.
I say "Yes," my Lord.
To the God of all justice:
I say "Yes," my Lord.
I say "Yes," my Lord.

REFRAIN
I say "Yes," my Lord, in all the good times,
through all the bad times,
I say "Yes," my Lord to every word
you speak.

2 Soy un sirviente del Señor:
Digo "Sí," Señor.
Digo "Sí," Señor.
y trabajo en los campos:
Digo "Sí," Señor.
Digo "Sí," Señor.
Soy un prisionero de sus guerras:
Digo "Sí," Señor.
Digo "Sí," Señor.
Como un político inevitable.
Digo "Sí," Señor.
Digo "Sí," Señor.

REFRAIN
Di go "Sí," Señor, en tiempos malos,
en tiempos buenos,
Di go "Sí," Señor a todo lo que hablas.

3 For the dream I have today:
I say "Yes," my Lord.
I say "Yes," my Lord.
To be a healer of all pain:
I say,"Yes," my Lord.
I say "Yes," my Lord.
To come to love my enemies:
I say "Yes," my Lord.
I say "Yes," my Lord.
For your peace in all the world:
I say "Yes," my Lord.
I say "Yes," my Lord.

REFRAIN
I say "Yes," my Lord, in all the good times,
through all the bad times,
I say "Yes," my Lord to every word
you speak.

4 Como Job incesantemente:
Digo "Sí," Señor.
Digo "Sí," Señor.
Como Maria completamente:
Digo "Sí," Señor.
Digo "Sí," Señor.
Como David enunacanción:
Digo "Sí," Señor.
Digo "Sí," Señor.
Como Israel, lleno deesperanza:
Digo "Sí," Señor.
Digo "Sí," Señor.

REFRAIN
Di go "Sí," Señor, en tiempos malos,
en tiempos buenos,
Di go "Sí," Señor a todo lo que hablas.

Words and Music: Donna Peña. © 1989 GIA Publications, Inc. All rights reserved.

Closing Song
HOW CAN WE NOT BUT SING
Donna Peña

1 La canción del amanecer, me inspira.
Canta mi corazón. La canción de la flor,
   Señor.
Canta mi alma. Rise above. Be part of.
Parte del gozo de creación.

2 En la noche, el ritmo de la cigarras,
Canta mi corazón.
¡Y el pulso del viento, sí! Canta mi alma.
Rise above. Be part of. Parte del gozo
   de creación. ¡Oh!

REFRAIN
How can we not but sing!
How can we not but praise you!
Here in my heart I'll never cease to
   sing to you day by day!

3 Cuando todo el pueblo canta de gozo
Canta mi corazón.
¡Y el cántico del Quetzal!
Canta mi alma.
Rise above. Be part of. Parte del gozo
   de creación. ¡Oh!

REFRAIN
How can we not but sing!
How can we not but praise you!
Here in my heart I'll never cease to
   sing to you day by day!

4 Cuando Mi Dios es muy compaisivo
   y bonito, misericordio
so y justiciero y ¡Sí, es maravilloso!
todas nuestras culpas y los pecados,
   los malvados, mi Dios perdonará.
¡Sí, es maravilloso!
Rise above. Be part of. Parte del gozo
   de creación. ¡Oh!

REFRAIN
How can we not but sing!
How can we not but praise you!
Here in my heart I'll never cease to
   sing to you day by day!
Por siempre cantaré.

*Words and Music: Donna Peña. © 1992 GIA
Publications, Inc. All rights reserved.*

Glossary

Assembly: When we, the believers, gather for worship we become the assembly. The *General Instruction of the Roman Missal* (2002) lists the four modes of Christ's presence in the Mass. It states that Christ is first present in the assembly, those gathered in his name. "Through Baptism and Confirmation the priestly people is enabled to celebrate the liturgy, while those of the faithful 'who have received Holy Orders, are appointed to nourish the Church with the word and grace of God in the name of Christ,' (*Lumen Gentium*, 11 § 2)" *Catechism of the Catholic Church, 1119.*

Chronos: Greek word for the chronological concept of time that is measured in years, months, weeks, days, hours, minutes, and seconds.

Collect: A short prayer given for a particular day, which the priest celebrant offers on behalf of the whole liturgical assembly following his invitation to pray ("Let us pray").

Congregation for Divine Worship and the Discipline of the Sacraments: A particular office of the Roman Curia that handles most affairs relating to liturgical practices of the Latin Church.

Consubstantial: A Christological term meaning "of one substance" first used by Tertullian to describe the relationship among the three persons of the Holy Trinity, who are eternal before all time and without end. The Son is begotten not made.

Council of Trent: This ecumenical council met on and off between 1545 and 1563 to address the Protestant Reformation and to define Church teachings in areas of dispute. The council issued numerous reform decrees. As a result of the Council, in 1570 Pope Pius V promulgated a new *Roman Missal* mandating the Tridentine Mass throughout the Western Church.

Dynamic equivalence: This theory of translation seeks to convey the essential meaning of the original text in the style and tone of the modern vernacular language.

Ecclesia, ekklesia: Latin and Greek terms for "church."

Formal equivalence: This theory of translation seeks to follow the syntax and vocabulary of the original language rendering the text word for word as closely as possible, in order to capture the original meaning.

Homooúsios: The Greek word ("same being" or "same essence") used by the Council of Nicea (325) to define the relationship of the Son to the Father. What is said of God the Father can be said of God the Son. It was made part of the Nicene Creed by the Council of Constantinople in 381. This is the Creed we most often proclaim on Sundays at Mass.

In Persona Christi: This Latin phrase refers to the role of the priest in the celebration of a sacrament. The priest acts "in the person of Christ." Each liturgy is a realization of the priestly office of Jesus Christ accomplished by the whole body of Christ.

Incarnate: God became fully human through the person of Jesus Christ; his divine nature was fully present at his conception.

International Commission on English in the Liturgy (ICEL): A joint commission of Catholic Bishops' Conferences in countries where English is used in the celebration of the Sacred Liturgy according to the Roman Rite. The commission's purpose is to prepare English translations of each of the Latin liturgical books and any individual liturgical texts in accord with the directives of the Holy See. Eleven conferences of bishops are full members of ICEL: Australia, Canada, England and Wales, India, Ireland, New Zealand, Pakistan, The Philippines, Scotland, South Africa, United States of America. There are 15 associate-member conferences of bishops.

Kairos: Greek word referring to the fullness of time when a particular event is to take place. We humans who are bound by time (*chronos*) are invited, through the liturgy, to experience the fullness of time (*kairos*).

Koinonia: This term is derived from the Greek term for communion. In the New Testament, it refers both to the relationship among the Christian community and to the sharing in the Eucharist.

Lectionary: The book containing the Scripture readings proclaimed at Mass (first reading from the Old Testament, or during Easter from certain books of the New Testament; responsorial Psalm; second reading from the New Testament Letters; and a Gospel reading). The readings recur in three-year cycle.

Liturgy: The public worship (prayer and ritual) for the service of others. Derived from the Greek *leitourgia* for *laos* (people) and *ergon* (work), to refer to the people's work or a public work done in service of others. In ancient Greek, it originally meant a duty of the cooperation of all citizens to make society work.

Liturgiam Authenticam: On the Use of Vernacular Languages in the Publication of Books of the Roman Liturgy. Issued March 28, 2001, this instruction from the Congregation for Divine Worship and the Discipline of the Sacraments that outlines the principles and rules for liturgical translation including more formal and literal translations of the original Latin texts.

Mediator Dei: Pope Pius XII's encyclical, published in 1947, emphasized the active participation of the faithful in the liturgy.

Paschal Mystery: The term used to designate the life, death, resurrection, and glorification of Jesus. Christ lived, died, is risen from the dead, and has returned in glory to his Father – not just for himself but for all God's creation and is the instrument of our salvation. Through this *pascha* of Jesus the church is born. All Christian liturgy is rooted in the paschal mystery of Jesus Christ.

Presider: A broad term referring to the leader of a liturgical rite. A presider may be ordained (priest, bishop or deacon) or lay. Only a bishop or priest presides at Eucharist. A deacon may preside at a wedding or baptism, while a lay person may preside for Liturgy of the Hours, a Liturgy of the Word, or a Sunday celebration in the absence of a priest.

Roman Missal: The liturgical book that contains the words and rubrics for the celebration of the Mass in the Roman Rite.

Sacramentary: Term formerly used for the book that contains the English translation of the Roman Missal; however, a true sacramentary contains all and only the words spoken (or sung) by the priest celebrant. The Sacramentary also provide the priest's texts at other occasions besides Mass.

Sacrosanctum Concilium **(*Constitution on the Sacred Liturgy*):** This first document of the Second Vatican Council provided an overarching theological groundwork of the importance of the liturgy in the Church, in the world, in the lives of the people and in the Mystical Union with Christ. The church is actualized and made manifest in liturgy, which anticipates the heavenly liturgy toward which we journey as pilgrims. It called for reform of the sacred liturgy to adapt to the signs of the times, including greater lay participation in the Church's liturgy and use of the vernacular. Promulgated by Paul VI on December 4, 1963.

Vernacular: The ordinary or everyday language of the people of a region.

Vox Clara: A new committee (Clear Voice) established by Pope John Paul II in 2002 to assist the Congregation for Divine Worship and the Discipline of the Sacraments in facilitating the new norms for translation with ICEL and the English-speaking Conferences of Bishops.

Lenten Resources from RENEW International

Lenten Longings, Years A, B, & C

Lent invites us to a time of prayer, reflection, and conversion. Make a six-week retreat by exploring the Sunday readings of Lent. Simple language and everyday metaphors steep you in the season's promptings to surrender self, work for justice, and deepen prayer life. *Lenten Longings* is well suited for seasonal groups, small Christian communities, and individual reflection. By Catherine T. Nerney, S.S.J., Ph.D.

- *Let Yourself Be ...* —Year A
- *For the Life of the World*—Year B
- *Seeing with God's Eyes*—Year C

Also available: companion music CD, prayer card, and downloadable parish invitation resources.

Reflexiones en Cuaresma, Años A, B, y C

Estas reflexiones sobre las lecturas dominicales de Cuaresma son un instrumento que tienen como objetivo contribuir a que, de manera sencilla, las personas que se reúnen en las pequeñas comunidades mediten sobre la Palabra de Dios. Además que durante este periodo sientan la fuerza de su mensaje y lo hagan parte de sus vidas. Por Dra. Irma Chávez.

- *Con Jesús vamos hacia la vida*—Año A
- *Llamados a la conversión*—Año B
- *Hacia el reino por la fe*—Año C

Disponível em Português
Reflexões na Quaresma, Anos A, B, e C

- *Com Jesus Rumo à Vida*—Ano A
- *Chamados à Conversão*—Ano B
- *Rumo ao Reino pela Fé*—Ano C

For these and the other fine faith-sharing resources from RENEW International presented on pages 53-60, please visit our secure online store: **www.renewintl.org/store**

For inquiries, contact us at

RENEW International
1232 George Street,
Plainfield, NJ 07062-1717

Telephone
(inquiries only):
908-769-5400

Toll free
(for orders only):
1-888-433-3221

Email:
Resources@renewintl.org

Strengthen Your Faith with...

WHY CATHOLIC?
Journey through the Catechism
A process of evangelization and adult faith formation

Would you like to deepen your understanding of the Catholic faith and gain the confidence to share it with others and live it in daily life? RENEW International recommends *WHY CATHOLIC? Journey through the Catechism*.

WHY CATHOLIC? Journey through the Catechism is a diocesan-wide, parish-based process of evangelization and adult faith formation from RENEW International. This process, designed for sharing in small Christian communities, is structured around exploring the important truths of our faith as they are presented in the *Catechism of the Catholic Church* and in the *United States Catholic Catechism for Adults*.

WHY CATHOLIC? helps nourish faith and enhance our sense of Catholic identity. The process and materials encourage us to understand and live the reasons why we are Catholic, and so lead us to a faith that is experienced more authentically, connecting us more deeply and meaningfully to God, and to others.

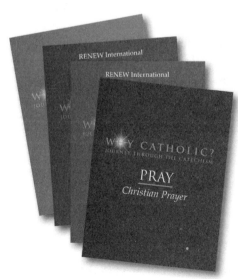

Faith-sharing Books

There are four books in the *WHY CATHOLIC?* series, each offering twelve sessions:

- *PRAY: Christian Prayer*
- *BELIEVE: Profession of Faith*
- *CELEBRATE: Sacraments*
- *LIVE: Christian Morality*

Song CD

For each of the four **WHY CATHOLIC?** books, there is a Song CD. Each CD is a 12-song compilation of the songs suggested for the moments of prayer during the faith-sharing sessions. The CDs are available singly, or as a set.

Companion Bulletins

Families can extend the fruits of the sharing on the same themes presented in the books by using *RENEWing Family Faith*: attractive four-color companion bulletins with activities and reflections for sharing among different age groups. Also available in Spanish.

A Complete Integrated Process

WHY CATHOLIC? is far more than printed resources for faith-sharing in small communities. It is a complete integrated process providing materials and support both in print and on the web, together with opportunities for faith enrichment events and retreats for the whole parish, as well as a series of training workshops for small community leaders.

Other Language Availability

This process of faith-building through faith-sharing is also available in Spanish: *¿POR QUÉ SER CATÓLICO?*

Please contact the RENEW International office for information about other language availabiltiy.

To learn more about bringing *WHY CATHOLIC? / ¿POR QUÉ SER CATÓLICO?* to your parish:

visit **www.whycatholic.org** or call at **908-769-5400**.

Center your life on Christ with...

ARISE Together in Christ
A parish-based process of evangelization and spiritual renewal

ARISE Together in Christ is a pastoral process that explores the spiritual standards of Christ in relation to all areas of life. Its scripturally grounded content emphasizes people living in good relationship with one another, as they make concrete applications of the gospel to daily live. *ARISE* begins with encountering Christ in Scripture and continues through life themes of conversion, justice, forgiveness, and reconciliation, culminating in the call to reach out as "Good News" to others.

The five Seasons of faith sharing in small Christian communities are central to the *ARISE Together in Christ* process.

For each Season, RENEW International offers a **faith-sharing book**, a **music CD** with the songs suggested in the faith-sharing book, and **downloadable resources** on our website for participating parishes.

The five Seasons are:

- *SEASON ONE: Encountering Christ Today*
- *SEASON TWO: Change Our Hearts*
- *SEASON THREE: In the Footsteps of Christ*
- *SEASON FOUR: New Heart, New Spirit*
- *SEASON FIVE: We Are the Good News!*

A Complete Integrated Process

For a complete, integrated experience of *ARISE Together in Christ*, RENEW International recommends using the resources as part of a comprehensive diocesan-wide, parish-based process that includes training for leaders, pastoral support and online tools and materials.

For more information, please visit **www. renewintl.org/arise** or call **908-769-5400**.

Other Faith-Sharing Resources from RENEW International

LONGING FOR THE HOLY:
Spirituality for Everyday Life
Based on selected insights of Ronald Rolheiser, O.M.I.

Experience how the gentle spiritual guidance and practical wisdom of best-selling Catholic author Fr. Ronald Rolheiser, O.M.I., can enliven everyday life. Suitable for small community faith sharing or individual reflection, *Longing for the Holy* covers different dimensions of contemporary spiritual life for those who want to enrich their sense of the presence of God and develop a deeper spirituality.

Faith-sharing Book

The Participant's Book contains twelve sessions with prayers, reflections, sharing questions, and stories from saints and contemporary people of faith.

Four-CD Set Audio Edition

This resource is also available as a four CD-set audio edition, which has both narrated text and songs for all twelve sessions.

Song CD

The songs suggested for the moments of prayer in the faith-sharing sessions are offered on this 13-song anthology CD.

The Kit

The Kit includes the essential ingredients to bring this engaging spiritual experience to your parish or small Christian community. Purchase of the kit provides membership benefits including the opportunity for web-based workshops, as well as a web library of support materials.

Other Language Availability

Ofrecemos también en español:
SEDIENTOS DE DIOS: Una espiritualidad para la gente de hoy
Doce sesiones, presentadas en dos libros de seis sesiones cada uno.

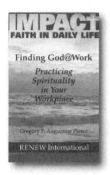

Finding God @ Work

Six faith-sharing sessions guide us on a quest: can God be found at work? If so, how? Examine your lived experience of work—both positively and negatively—from a spiritual vantage point, considering relevant passages from Scripture, and principles of Catholic social teaching. By Greg F. Augustine Pierce

Forgiveness and Reconciliation

The insightful wisdom and many inspiring stories of forgiveness and reconciliation offer a profound understanding of people's desire to be forgiven and the steps to take to live reconciled lives. Reflect on the healing power of God and the richness of the sacrament of reconciliation to discover again how to live in the freedom of God. By Jeanne Marie Hiesberger

SOWING SEEDS
Essentials for Small Community Leaders

This book offers a comprehensive collection of pastoral insights and practical suggestions to help small community leaders guide their groups in a way that nourishes spiritual growth. Culled from RENEW International's three decades of experience in pioneering and promoting small Christian communities, this book overflows with simple but effective ideas and strategies that will enhance the way these groups reflect on and respond to the Gospel.

For more information or to order, please visit our secure online store at **www.renewintl.org/store** or use our toll free order line: **1-888-433-3221**.

También disponible en español:
SEMBRADORES DE SEMILLAS
Guía para un peregrinaje espiritual
Una magnífica guía que detalla paso por paso cómo iniciar y sostener el compartir de la fe en su comunidad.